NATIONAL GEOGRAPHIC

CALIFORNIA

WORLD HISTORY

MEDIEVAL AND
EARLY MODERN TIMES

CALIFORNIA
KNOWLEDGE, CONCEPTS, AND SKILLS

Every Day for Every Student

- Social Studies Skills Reading and Writing Lessons
- Reading and Note-Taking
- Vocabulary Practice
- Biographies
- Document-Based Question Templates

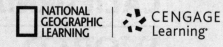

Acknowledgments

Grateful acknowledgment is given to the authors, artists, photographers, museums, publishers, and agents for permission to reprint copyrighted material. Every effort has been made to secure the appropriate permission. If any omissions have been made or if corrections are required, please contact the Publisher.

Photographic Credits

Cover: ©Michael Melford/National Geographic Creative

"National Geographic", "National Geographic Society" and the Yellow Border Design are registered trademarks of the National Geographic Society ® Marcas Registradas

For product information and technology assistance, contact us at Customer & Sales Support, 888-915-3276

For permission to use material from this text or product, submit all requests online at **www.cengage.com/permissions**

Further permissions questions can be emailed to **permissionrequest@cengage.com**

National Geographic Learning | Cengage
1 N. State Street, Suite 900
Chicago, IL 60602

Cengage Learning is a leading provider of customized learning solutions with employees residing in nearly 40 different countries and sales in more than 125 countries around the world. Find your local representative at **www.cengage.com.**

Visit National Geographic Learning online at **NGL.Cengage.com/school**

Visit our corporate website at **www.cengage.com**

ISBN: 978-13377-0004-7

Printed in the United States of America

Print Number: 08
Print Year: 2020

WORLD HISTORY KNOWLEDGE AND CONCEPTS

UNIT 1

CHAPTER 1 SECTION 1
The Empire at Its Height

NATIONAL GEOGRAPHIC LEARNING

READING AND NOTE-TAKING

ORGANIZE INFORMATION Use the table below to organize information about the legacy of Rome after you read Section 1.

Category	Legacy	Examples
Language	Latin became very influential, it became the source of other languages, and English borrowed words from it.	French the word campus prefixes and suffixes in English
Literature		
Philosophy		
Art		

Category	Legacy	Examples
Architecture		
Law and Government		
Engineering		

Chapter 1 SECTION 1 **ACTIVITY A** **WORLD HISTORY**

**NATIONAL
GEOGRAPHIC
LEARNING**

READING AND NOTE-TAKING

IDENTIFY HISTORICAL FIGURES After you read Section 2, use the descriptions below to identify historical figures involved in early Christianity. Write the name of the person that matches each description. You may use the names of some figures more than once.

Christianity is centered on his teachings. _____

He blamed the great fire of Rome
on the Christians. _____

He was the first Roman emperor who
converted to Christianity. _____

He wrote epistles explaining
Jesus' teachings. _____

He included the Parable of the
Good Samaritan in his gospel. _____

He was born into a poor family
around 6 B.C. _____

He sentenced Jesus to die by crucifixion. _____

He was killed in a Roman massacre
of Christians in A.D. 64. _____

He made Christianity the official
religion of Rome. _____

He used parables to teach. _____

They were Jesus' closest followers
who helped spread his teachings. _____

UNIT 1 CHAPTER 1 SECTION 2
Christianity

READING AND NOTE-TAKING

INTERPRET MAPS   After you read Section 2, review the map in Lesson 2.2
and use it to answer the questions below.

What is the title of the map? _____

_____

What do the orange areas on the map represent? _____

_____

What do the yellow areas on the map represent? _____

_____

What do the largest orange areas have in common? _____

_____

_____

About how long did it take for Christianity to spread through the empire? _____

_____

_____

How would you describe the expansion of Christianity during this time? _____

_____

_____

What area to the east of the empire was largely untouched by Christianity? _____

_____

_____

What generalizations can you make about the spread of Christianity in the Roman Empire?

_____

_____

UNIT 1

CHAPTER 1 SECTION 3
Decline and Fall

READING AND NOTE-TAKING

<u>MAKE GENERALIZATIONS</u>   After you finish reading about the fall of the Roman Empire in Section 3, read these excerpts from the text. Then, using your own words, write one or two generalizations about each excerpt.

1. **Excerpt:** "At its height, the Roman Empire stretched from Scotland to the Sahara, an area about half the size of the United States. This vast expanse, with huge geographic and cultural differences, was very difficult to govern effectively. Defending such a large area also proved difficult."

   Generalization: Large geographic areas are difficult to govern and to defend against invaders.

2. **Excerpt:** "Constant warfare also ruined the economy. Trade was interrupted, and the empire had to rely on its inadequate agricultural resources. The people suffered food shortages and higher taxes."

   Generalization:

UNIT 1

CHAPTER 1 SECTION 3
Decline and Fall *continued*

NATIONAL
GEOGRAPHIC
LEARNING

3. **Excerpt:** "Diocletian had a radical plan: In A.D. 285, he divided the empire in two. Diocletian ruled the Eastern Roman Empire, and his trusted friend Maximian ruled the Western Roman Empire. Each man appointed a junior emperor to rule with him."

Generalization:

4. **Excerpt:** "Diocletian and Constantine only delayed the end of the Western Roman Empire. The end came in the form of barbarians, a Greek word Romans used to describe all people outside of the empire."

Generalization:

Chapter 1 SECTION 3 **ACTIVITY A** WORLD HISTORY

UNIT 1

CHAPTER 1 SECTION 1
The Empire at Its Height

VOCABULARY PRACTICE

KEY VOCABULARY

- **aqueduct** (AK-wih-duhkt) *n.* a long stone channel that carries clean water

- **arch** *n.* a curved structure over an opening

- **emperor** (EHM-puh-ruhr) *n.* the supreme ruler of an empire

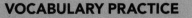

RELATED IDEA WEB   Write one of the Key Vocabulary words inside a circle, along with its definition in your own words. Then draw lines or arrows connecting the circles to show how the words are related, based on what you read in Section 1. Write your explanation of the connection next to the line or arrow.

emperor _____

_____

_____

_____

_____

_____

_____

_____

_____

_____

_____

_____

_____

UNIT 1

CHAPTER 1 SECTION 1
The Empire at Its Height

VOCABULARY PRACTICE

KEY VOCABULARY

- **bas-relief** (bah ruh-LEEF) *n.* a realistic sculpture with figures raised against a flat background

- **fresco** (FREHS-koh) *n.* a picture painted directly onto a wall

- **mosaic** (moh-ZAY-ick) *n.* a grouping of tiny colored stone cubes set in mortar to create a picture or design

- **oratory** (OHR-uh-tohr-ee) *n.* the art of public speaking

WORDS IN CONTEXT   Follow the directions for using the Key Vocabulary words in context.

1. Explain what *oratory* is and describe its value in ancient Rome.

_____

_____

_____

_____

2. Explain what a *bas-relief* is and where you might see one today.

_____

_____

_____

_____

3. Describe what a *mosaic* is.

_____

_____

_____

_____

4. Explain what a *fresco* is, and how frescoes were used.

_____

_____

_____

_____

UNIT 1

CHAPTER 1 SECTION 2
Christianity

NATIONAL GEOGRAPHIC LEARNING

VOCABULARY PRACTICE

KEY VOCABULARY

- **catacomb** (KA-tuh-kohm) *n.* a hidden underground chamber where people are buried

- **epistle** (ih-PIH-suhl) *n.* a letter

- **missionary** (MIH-shuh-nair-ee) *n.* a person who goes to another country to do religious work; a person who tries to spread Christianity to others

- **parable** (PAIR-uh-buhl) *n.* in the Bible, a short story about everyday life

- **pope** *n.* the leader of the Roman Catholic Church

WORD SQUARE   Complete a Word Square for the Key Vocabulary words.

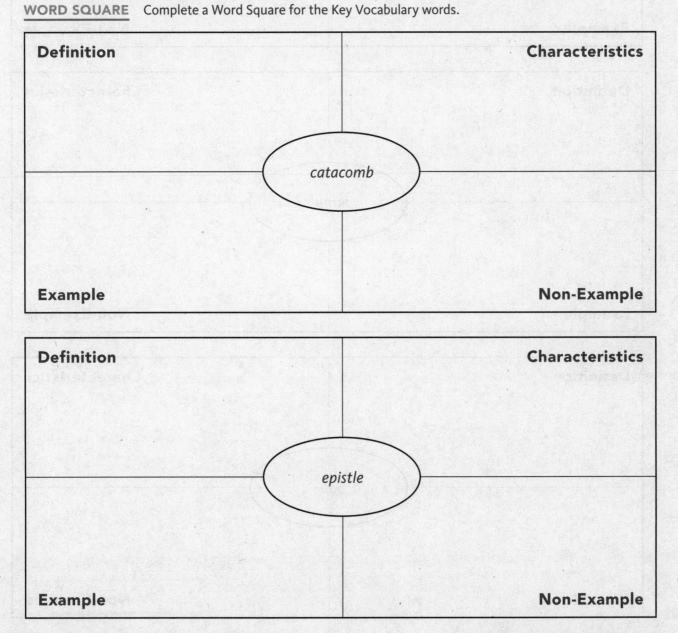

Definition	Characteristics
	catacomb
Example	Non-Example

Definition	Characteristics
	epistle
Example	Non-Example

UNIT **1** CHAPTER 1 SECTION 2
Christianity *continued*

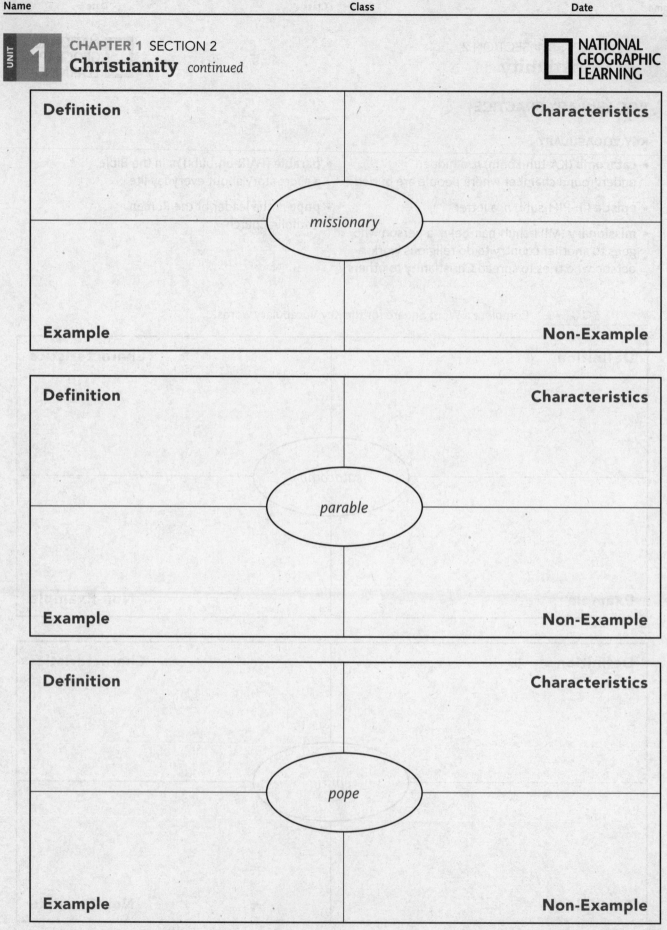

Definition	Characteristics
	missionary
Example	**Non-Example**

Definition	Characteristics
	parable
Example	**Non-Example**

Definition	Characteristics
	pope
Example	**Non-Example**

UNIT 1 CHAPTER 1 SECTION 3
Decline and Fall

VOCABULARY PRACTICE

KEY VOCABULARY

- **barbarian** (bahr-BAIR-ee-uhn) *n.* in this context, a person who lived outside the Roman Empire

WORD MAP   Complete a Word Map for the Key Vocabulary word.

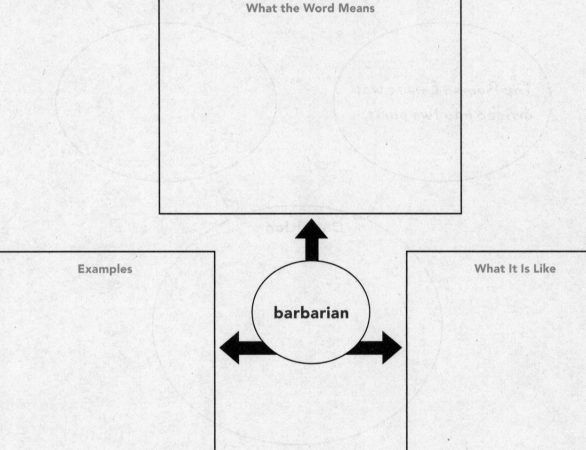

What the Word Means

Examples

barbarian

What It Is Like

Summarize   Write a sentence explaining who the barbarians were and what effect they had on the Roman Empire.

_____

_____

_____

_____

Decline and Fall

NATIONAL GEOGRAPHIC LEARNING

VOCABULARY PRACTICE

KEY VOCABULARY

- **tetrarchy** (TEH-trahr-kee) *n.* a system of rule by four emperors

VOCABULARY CLUSTER   Complete the Vocabulary Cluster below for the Key Vocabulary word *tetrarchy*. Write the definition in the center.

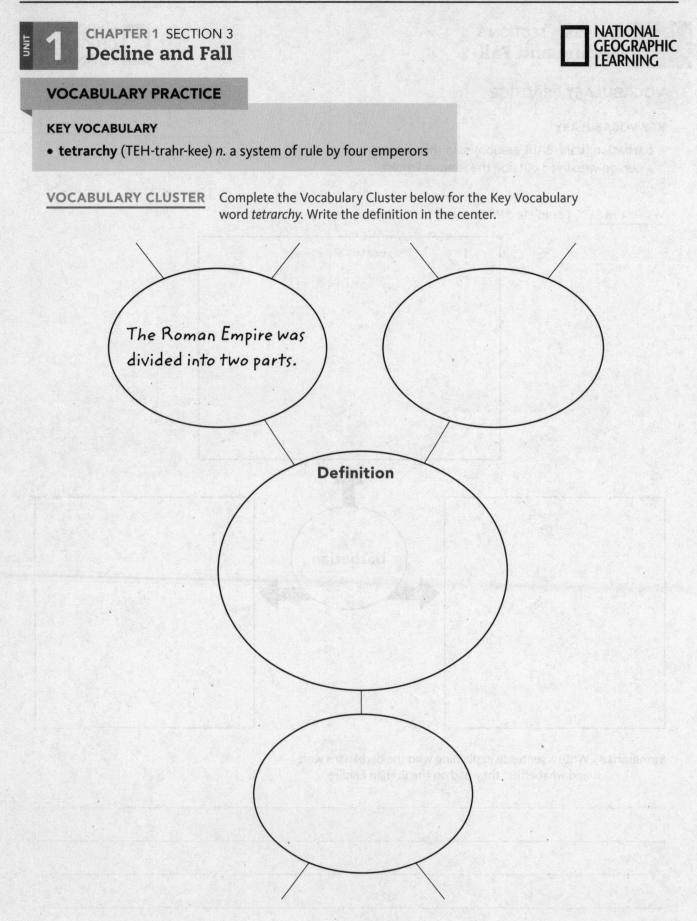

The Roman Empire was divided into two parts.

Definition

UNIT 1 BIOGRAPHY

PAUL

Paul, also known as Saul of Tarsus, is considered one of the most influential early Christian missionaries and church leaders. His letters, which make up several books of the New Testament, helped shaped early Christianity.

- **Job:** Tent Maker, Apostle
- **Notable Moment:** Conversion to Christianity
- **Skill:** Epistle Writing

Paul was born around A.D. 10 in the city of Tarsus, located in present-day Turkey. He was a well-educated Jew and a Roman citizen. According to his writings in the New Testament, Paul was a tent maker by trade.

Paul was brought up to strictly follow the Jewish laws, and he did so with zeal. At first, he was an enemy of early Christianity. He spent much of the first half of his life traveling to synagogues, arresting and persecuting people involved in the growing Christian movement.

According to Paul's own account, he converted to Christianity while on the road to Damascus to visit the synagogues there. He claimed that on his journey, a bright light shone on him and he had a vision in which Jesus revealed himself as the Son of God. The incident changed Paul, and from that time on, he began spreading Jesus' teachings. Paul had never met Jesus, so he sought out Peter, an apostle of Jesus, to learn how Jesus lived.

Paul traveled throughout Asia Minor and Greece, gaining converts and setting up churches. He wrote letters, called epistles, which explained Jesus' teachings. His epistles, originally written in Greek, make up 13 of the

Mosaic of Paul (A.D. 10 – A.D. 64) in Chora Church, Istanbul, Turkey

27 books of the New Testament. The epistles were sent to early churches and individuals and they included explanations of the gospels, solutions to local problems in the churches, and advice on how to live a Christian life. The letters were not originally intended to be a treatise on Christianity, but they became so over time.

When Paul returned to Jerusalem with a group of converts in the late A.D. 50s, he was arrested and imprisoned. Because he was a Roman citizen, he was sent to a prison in Rome. Roman leaders realized that Christianity had become popular. They feared this new religion posed a threat to the Roman Empire, so they made Christianity illegal. The Romans, likely in a mass execution of Christians, killed Paul in A.D. 64.

REVIEW & ASSESS

1. **Analyze Cause and Effect** What caused Paul to convert to Christianity?

_____

_____

2. **Draw Conclusions** How did Paul's epistles help spread the teachings of Jesus?

_____

_____

Pantheon/Superstock

UNIT **1**

BIOGRAPHY
ATTILA

Attila, king of the Huns, was one of the most notorious of the barbarian rulers. Using cunning threats and ferocious fighting methods, Attila and the Huns attacked both the Western and Eastern Roman Empires. Though there are no records describing his qualities as a leader, some argue that his many military successes show that he was an outstanding military commander.

Illustration of Attila (A.D. 406–A.D. 453) invading northern Italy with his Huns

- **Job:** King of the Huns
- **Arch Enemies:** Romans, Visigoths
- **Talents:** Invading, Conquering

Not much is known about Attila's early life. Some believe that he was born in the area that is present-day Hungary around A.D. 406. During the fifth century, the Huns ruled a large empire. Attila ruled as king of the Huns from 434 to 453. He ruled with his brother, Bleda, until 445, when Attila murdered Bleda and became the sole ruler.

At the time of Attila's rule, the Western Roman Empire was disintegrating. Invasions by several barbarian tribes added to the instability. The Eastern Roman Empire and its capital in Constantinople were stronger and more stable. To keep from being attacked by the Huns, the Eastern emperor signed a treaty with Attila and his brother in which he agreed to pay 700 pounds of gold tribute each year.

However, when the Eastern Romans failed to keep up the payments, Attila attacked the empire in 441 and again in 443. The attacks resulted in the Eastern Roman Empire losing much of its land in southeastern Europe. Attila also demanded that the Eastern Romans pay the tribute that was owed, and then he tripled future tributes to 2,100 pounds of gold each year.

In 451, Attila turned his attention to Gaul, or present-day France. He wanted to reclaim the land that the Visigoths, one of the Germanic tribes, had conquered. In the meantime the powerful Roman general Aetius allied himself with Theodoric I, the king of the Visigoths. They combined their forces against Attila and the Huns and forced them to withdraw. This was Attila's only defeat.

Two years after that defeat, Attila planned to attack the Eastern Roman Empire. The emperor there had refused to pay the tribute that Attila demanded. However, the night before the planned attack, Attila died in his sleep.

REVIEW & ASSESS

1. **Analyze Cause and Effect** What effect did the Eastern Roman emperor's failure to pay tribute to Attila have on the Eastern Roman Empire?

_____

_____

2. **Make Inferences** Why do you think Attila was considered an outstanding military commander?

_____

_____

CHAPTER 1 LESSON 2.3
Writings from the New Testament

DOCUMENT-BASED QUESTION

Use the questions here to help you analyze the sources and write your paragraph.

DOCUMENT ONE: The Parable of the Good Samaritan

1A According to this parable, how should we answer the question "Who is my neighbor?"?

_____

_____

_____

1B Constructed Response How does the Samaritan's response to the beaten man differ from the responses of the priest and Levite?

_____

_____

_____

DOCUMENT TWO: from Paul's Epistle to the Galatians

2A According to Paul, what makes all people "sons of God"?

_____

_____

_____

_____

2B Constructed Response What important Christian ideas is Paul stating in this epistle?

_____

_____

_____

_____

SYNTHESIZE & WRITE

What are some fundamental Christian ideas about how people should treat one another?

Topic Sentence: _____

_____

Your Paragraph: _____

_____

_____

_____

_____

_____

© National Geographic Learning, Cengage Learning

READING AND NOTE-TAKING

IDENTIFY PROBLEMS AND ADVANTAGES As you read Section 1, use the table below to take notes on the problems and advantages faced in the Byzantine Empire following the fall of Rome.

Problems	Advantages
Open to attack	Well situated for trade

UNIT 1

CHAPTER 2 SECTION 1
The Early Empire

NATIONAL GEOGRAPHIC LEARNING

READING AND NOTE-TAKING

SEQUENCE NAME CHANGES   As you read Section 1, notice the series of name changes that affected Byzantium and the Roman Empire after the division of the Roman Empire. Keep track of these changes using the boxes below. Include details of who changed the names, when, and why.

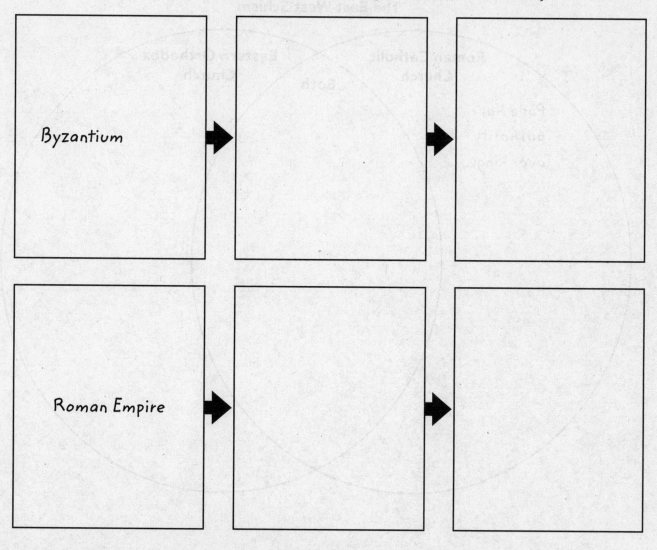

Byzantium ➤   ➤

Roman Empire ➤   ➤

Make Inferences   What might be one reason a leader might change the name of a city or an empire?

_____

_____

_____

UNIT 1

CHAPTER 2 SECTION 2
The Later Empire

NATIONAL
GEOGRAPHIC
LEARNING

READING AND NOTE-TAKING

COMPARE AND CONTRAST Use the Venn Diagram below to compare and contrast the Roman Catholic Church and Eastern Orthodox Church as you read Lesson 2.1.

The East-West Schism

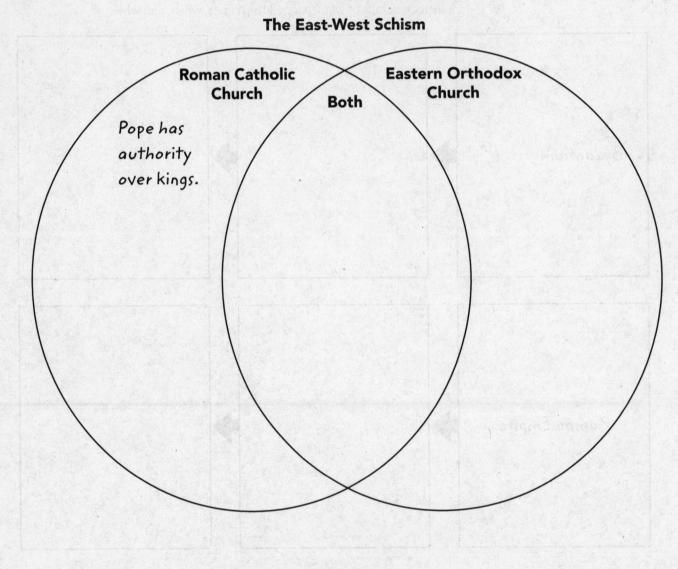

Roman Catholic Church

Both

Eastern Orthodox Church

Pope has authority over kings.

UNIT **1** CHAPTER 2 SECTION 2
The Later Empire

READING AND NOTE-TAKING

IDENTIFY MAIN IDEA AND DETAILS Preview Lesson 2.3 by looking at the painting. Then complete the chart with details about the text and painting. Finally, write the main idea of the lesson in your own words.

2.3 The End of an Empire

Interpret Visuals Based on the painting in Lesson 2.3, what do you think this lesson might be about?

_____

_____

Details: Debts and Invasions	Details: New Golden Age and Fall	Details: Painting
After Justinian's death, the plague made a comeback.		

Main Idea

_____

_____

_____

UNIT 1   **CHAPTER 2** SECTION 1
The Early Empire

NATIONAL GEOGRAPHIC LEARNING

VOCABULARY PRACTICE

KEY VOCABULARY

- **crossroads** *n.* the place where two roads meet
- **diversity** (dy-VUHR-suh-tee) *n.* a range of different things; a variety

VOCABULARY Y-CHART   Complete a Y-Chart to compare the meanings of the vocabulary words *crossroads* and *diversity*.

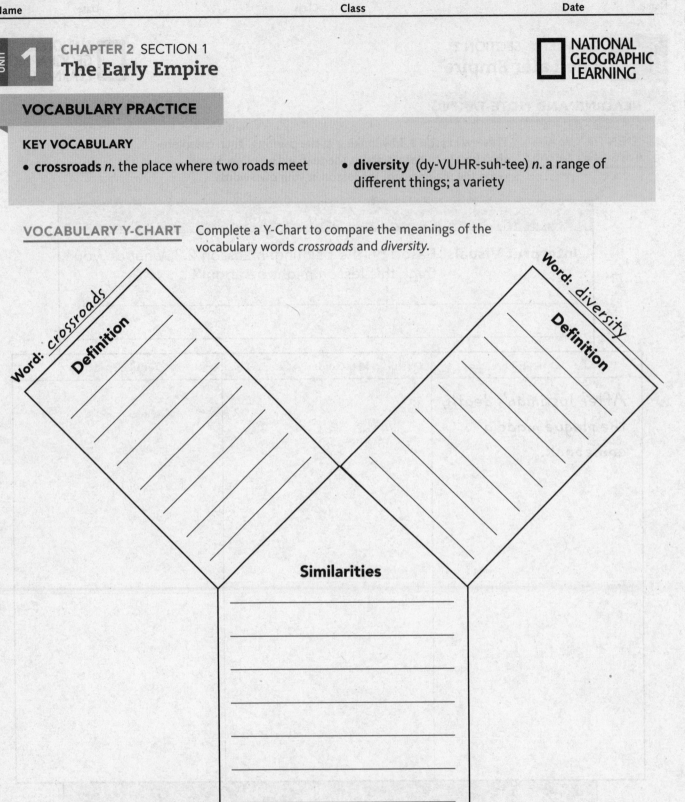

Word: *crossroads*

Definition

Word: *diversity*

Definition

Similarities

CHAPTER 2 SECTION 1
The Early Empire

NATIONAL GEOGRAPHIC LEARNING

VOCABULARY PRACTICE

KEY VOCABULARY

- **divine** (DEE-vyne) *adj*. having the nature of a god

- **heresy** (HAIR-uh-see) *n*. beliefs contrary to Church teachings; opposition to Church policy

DEFINITION MAP   Complete a Definition Map for each Key Vocabulary word.

WORD   DEFINITION   SENTENCE

divine

EXAMPLE

WORD   DEFINITION   SENTENCE

heresy

EXAMPLE

Chapter 2 SECTION 1 **ACTIVITY B**   WORLD HISTORY

CHAPTER 2 SECTION 2
The Later Empire

NATIONAL GEOGRAPHIC LEARNING

VOCABULARY PRACTICE

KEY VOCABULARY

- **creed** *n.* a statement of belief
- **excommunicate** (ECKS-kah-myoon-uh-kate) *v.* to officially exclude a member of a church from its rituals and membership
- **icon** (EYE-kawn) *n.* an image of Jesus or a saint
- **patriarch** (PAY-tree-arkh) *n.* the leader of the Eastern Orthodox Church
- **schism** (SKIH-zuhm) *n.* a separation

TRAVEL ARTICLE Imagine you are a travel writer traveling across Turkey and taking a tour of Hagia Sophia. Use details from Section 2 to retell the history you learned during your tour about how the church divided. Use all of the Key Vocabulary words in your article.

Article Title: _____

Date: _____

_____

_____

_____

_____

_____

_____

_____

_____

_____

_____

_____

_____

_____

_____

_____

_____

_____

_____

© National Geographic Learning, Cengage Learning

UNIT 1

CHAPTER 2 SECTION 2
The Later Empire

NATIONAL GEOGRAPHIC LEARNING

VOCABULARY PRACTICE

KEY VOCABULARY

- **creed** *n.* a statement of belief

- **excommunicate** (ECKS-kah-myoon-uh-kate) *v.* to officially exclude a member of a church from its rituals and membership

- **icon** (EYE-kawn) *n.* an image of Jesus or a saint

- **patriarch** (PAY-tree-arkh) *n.* the leader of the Eastern Orthodox Church

- **schism** (SKIH-zuhm) *n.* a separation

THREE-COLUMN CHART   Complete the chart for each of the five Key Vocabulary words. Write the word and its definition. Then provide a definition using your own words.

Word	Definition	In My Own Words

Chapter 2 SECTION 2 **ACTIVITY B**   WORLD HISTORY

Empress Theodora with her court of two ministers and seven women, detail of Theodora, c.547 A.D. (mosaic) (detail of 220592 & 244980), Byzantine School, (6th century) / San Vitale, Ravenna, Italy / Bridgeman Images

UNIT **1** BIOGRAPHY

THEODORA

Theodora, the empress of the Byzantine Empire, was a trusted adviser to her husband and co-ruler, Justinian I. She was also powerful in her own right and influential in much of the legislation passed during Justinian's reign.

- **Job:** Byzantine Empress
- **Characteristics:** Intelligent, Persuasive
- **Co-Ruler:** Justinian

Not much is known about Theodora's early life. She was born in A.D. 497 to a poor family. Her father was a bear keeper for a circus in Constantinople. At one point in her youth, Theodora made a living as an actress and also as a wool spinner.

Theodora's beauty and superior intelligence attracted Justinian, who married her in 525. Her strong and persuasive personality prepared her well for her role as empress. Theodora influenced nearly all the laws passed under Justinian's rule, and Justinian considered her his co-ruler. Theodora demonstrated skill in handling political affairs, including receiving and corresponding with foreign leaders—two duties previously performed only by the emperor.

Throughout his reign, Justinian sought and generally followed Theodora's advice. During the Nika riots in 532, for example, two political groups banded together to oppose the government and install their own emperor. Justinian's advisors urged him to leave. Theodora, however, counseled Justinian to stay and keep his empire

Detail of a Byzantine mosaic of Theodora (A.D. 497–A.D. 565)

intact. Justinian took Theodora's advice. His generals then gathered the rebel groups and executed them.

Some of Theodora's most important accomplishments concerned protecting different groups in the empire. She introduced laws that enhanced women's rights, including laws that provided greater benefits for women after divorce. She also worked to protect religious freedoms in the empire, and she demonstrated charity with the poor. For these reasons, Theodora is frequently portrayed as a heroine and a champion for the less-fortunate.

When Theodora died in 548, Justinian was devastated by her death. Historians have noted that very few laws were enacted between the time of her death and Justinian's death in 565.

REVIEW & ASSESS

1. **Summarize** In what ways did Empress Theodora demonstrate her skills in politics and foreign affairs?

_____

_____

2. **Make Inferences** What does the fact that very few laws were passed after Theodora's death say about her political influence?

_____

_____

UNIT 1 — CHAPTER 3 SECTION 1
The Roots of Islam

READING AND NOTE-TAKING

MAKE GENERALIZATIONS   In the boxes below, write general statements that summarize the most important events in Lessons 1.1, 1.2, 1.3, and 1.5. Under each lesson title, write the subsection head before you write your general statements.

1.1 Trading Crossroads

Desert Life

Early tribes of nomadic herders first inhabited the Arabian Peninsula.

Growth of Cities

1.2 The Prophet of Islam

NATIONAL
GEOGRAPHIC
LEARNING

1.3 Beliefs and Laws

1.5 After Muhammad

READING AND NOTE-TAKING

COMPARE AND CONTRAST   As you read Lessons 2.1 and 2.2, use a Venn Diagram to take notes on the similarities and differences between the Umayyads and the Abbasids. Then answer the question below.

Umayyads   **Abbasids**

Both

Damascus

Compare and Contrast   In what ways did the Umayyads and Abbasids differ from each other?

_____

_____

_____

_____

CHAPTER 3 SECTION 2
Muslim Empires

READING AND NOTE-TAKING

SEQUENCE EVENTS   After reading Lesson 2.4, complete a Sequence Chain that shows the major periods and events that occurred during the rise and fall of the Ottoman Empire. Sequence the periods and events in chronological order.

Ottoman Empire

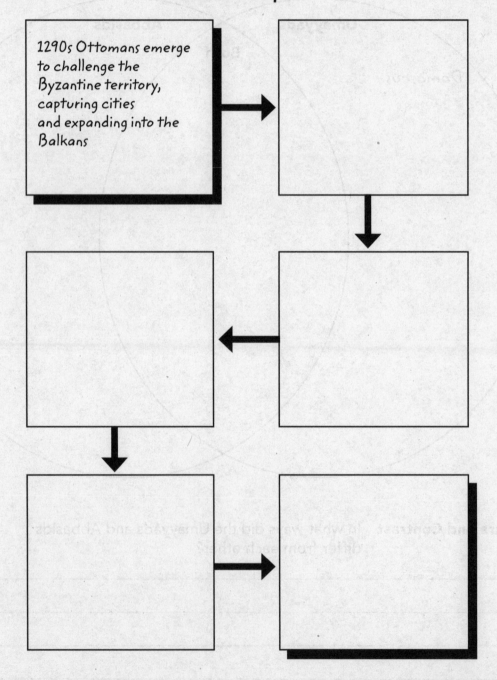

1290s Ottomans emerge to challenge the Byzantine territory, capturing cities and expanding into the Balkans

Chapter 3 SECTION 2 **ACTIVITY B**   WORLD HISTORY

UNIT 1

CHAPTER 3 SECTION 3
The Islamic Cultural Legacy

READING AND NOTE-TAKING

IDENTIFY INNOVATIONS As you read Section 3, complete the circles in the Idea Web with notes about Islamic innovations in literature, mathematics, philosophy, and architecture. Add extra spokes and circles as needed.

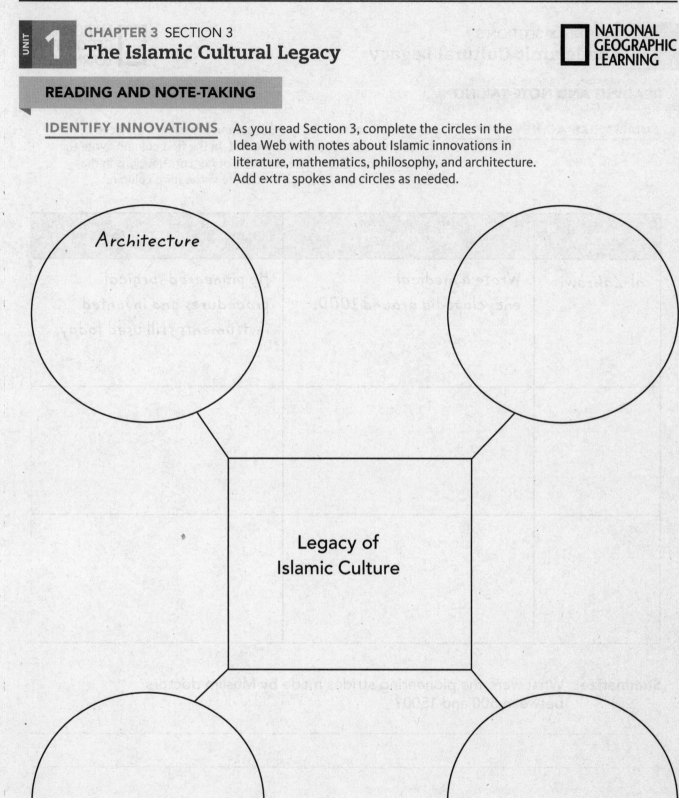

Architecture

Legacy of
Islamic Culture

UNIT 1

CHAPTER 3 SECTION 3
The Islamic Cultural Legacy

NATIONAL
GEOGRAPHIC
LEARNING

READING AND NOTE-TAKING

SUMMARIZE ACHIEVEMENTS   As you read Lessons 3.1 and 3.2, summarize Islamic medical achievements, both past and present. In the first column, write the person's name. Then write about his or her contributions in the second column and a specific example in the third column.

Person	Contribution	Example
al-Zahrawi	Wrote a medical encyclopedia around 1000.	He pioneered surgical procedures and invented instruments still used today.

Summarize   What were the pioneering strides made by Muslim doctors between 500 and 1500?

_____

_____

_____

_____

_____

UNIT 1

CHAPTER 3 SECTION 1
The Roots of Islam

NATIONAL GEOGRAPHIC LEARNING

VOCABULARY PRACTICE

KEY VOCABULARY

- **caliph** (KAY-lihf) *n.* the title of the chief Muslim leader who was regarded as a successor of Muhammad
- **clan** *n.* a group of families that shares a common ancestor
- **imam** (ih-MAHM) *n.* a Muslim religious leader

- **mosque** (MAHSK) *n.* a Muslim place of worship
- **oasis** (oh-AY-sihs) *n.* a fertile place with water in a desert
- **pilgrimage** (PIHL-gruh-mihj) *n.* a journey to a holy place
- **prophet** *n.* a teacher believed to be inspired by God
- **shari'a** (shah-REE-ah) *n.* an Islamic system of law that covers all aspects of human behavior

DEFINITION TREE For each Key Vocabulary word in the Tree Diagrams below, write the definition on the top branch and then use each word in a sentence.

caliph

Definition

the title of the chief Muslim leader who was regarded as

a successor of Muhammad

Sentence

_____

_____

clan

Definition

_____

Sentence

_____

_____

imam

Definition

_____

Sentence

_____

_____

mosque

Definition

_____

_____

Sentence

_____

_____

oasis

Definition

_____

_____

Sentence

_____

_____

pilgrimage

Definition

_____

_____

Sentence

_____

_____

prophet

Definition

_____

_____

Sentence

_____

_____

shari'a

Definition

_____

_____

Sentence

_____

_____

Chapter 3 SECTION 1 **ACTIVITY A** WORLD HISTORY

UNIT 1

CHAPTER 3 SECTION 2
Muslim Empires

VOCABULARY PRACTICE

KEY VOCABULARY

- **bureaucracy** (byoo-RAH-krah-see) *n.* a system of government in which appointed officials in specialized departments run the various offices

- **janissary** (JAN-uhs-air-ee) *n.* a highly trained and disciplined soldier in the Ottoman army

- **mercenary** (MUHR-suhn-air-ee) *n.* a hired soldier

- **shah** *n.* a ruler of the Safavid Empire; the Persian title for "king"

- **sultan** (SUHL-tuhn) *n.* a ruler of the Ottoman Empire

- **tolerance** *n.* the sympathy for the beliefs and practices of others

I READ, I KNOW, AND SO   Complete the charts below for the Key Vocabulary words in Section 2. Write down the sentence in which the word appears. Then write down what else you read about the word. Finally, draw a conclusion about the word based on what you have learned.

I Read

The Umayyads set up an efficient bureaucracy to govern the Muslim empire.

	bureaucracy	
I Know		**And So**

I Read

	janissary	
I Know		**And So**

UNIT **1**

CHAPTER 3 SECTION 2
Muslim Empires *continued*

**NATIONAL
GEOGRAPHIC
LEARNING**

I Read		
I Know	**mercenary**	**And So**

I Read		
I Know	**shah**	**And So**

I Read		
I Know	**sultan**	**And So**

I Read		
I Know	**tolerance**	**And So**

UNIT 1

CHAPTER 3 SECTION 3
Islamic Cultural Legacy

NATIONAL GEOGRAPHIC LEARNING

VOCABULARY PRACTICE

KEY VOCABULARY

- **arabesque** (air-uh-BESK) *n.* an abstract design made up of patterns or flowers, leaves, vines, or geometric shapes

- **calligraphy** (kuh-LIH-gruh-fee) *n.* a form of elegant writing

- **medieval** (mihd-EE-vuhl) *adj.* a period in history that spanned from the A.D. 500s to the 1500s; from the Latin *medium* (middle) and *aevum* (age)

- **minaret** (min-uh-REHT) *n.* a tall, slender tower that is part of a mosque

FOUR-COLUMN CHART Complete a Four-Column Chart for the Key Vocabulary words in Section 3. In the last column, use the word in a sentence.

Word	Definition	Illustration	Sentence
arabesque			Mosques often feature designs such as arabesques.

UNIT 1

CHAPTER 3 SECTION 3
Islamic Cultural Legacy

VOCABULARY PRACTICE

KEY VOCABULARY

- **arabesque** (air-uh-BEHSK) *n.* an abstract design made up of patterns or flowers, leaves, vines, or geometric shapes

- **calligraphy** (kuh-LIH-gruh-fee) *n.* a form of elegant writing

- **medieval** (mihd-EE-vuhl) *adj.* a period in history that spanned from the A.D. 500s to the 1500s; from the Latin *medium* (middle) and *aevum* (age)

- **minaret** (min-uh-REHT) *n.* a tall, slender tower that is part of a mosque

DESCRIPTIVE PARAGRAPH Write a descriptive paragraph about buildings and architecture in medieval Islamic civilization. Be sure to use all the Key Vocabulary words in Section 3.

_____

_____

_____

_____

_____

_____

_____

_____

_____

_____

_____

_____

_____

_____

_____

_____

UNIT 1 BIOGRAPHY

KHADIJAH

Khadijah was the first wife of Muhammad. She was a successful and wealthy merchant, and she was Muhammad's first convert to Islam.

- **Job:** Merchant
- **Qualities:** Generosity, Compassion, Loyalty
- **Home:** Mecca

Khadijah was born around A.D. 556 in Mecca, in what is today Saudi Arabia. She had been married and widowed twice before she met Muhammad and had children in each of the marriages. Her first husband was a wealthy merchant, and when he died Khadijah continued his trading business. Her business was successful and became known throughout the Arabian Peninsula. Khadijah had a reputation for being generous, sharing her wealth, and caring for the poor.

With her successful business booming, Khadijah soon realized that she needed someone to work as her agent on the caravans that traveled between Mecca and present-day Syria. She met and hired Muhammad, who had gained a reputation for being intelligent and honest. He worked out well as her agent. Khadijah, impressed by his qualities, thought Muhammad would be a suitable husband and soon asked him to marry her. She is believed to have been 15 years older than Muhammad, but some people think she might have been younger than that. Khadijah and Muhammad had six children together—two sons and four daughters. The two sons died as young children.

When Muhammad described his revelations from Gabriel, who in Islam is God's messenger, Khadijah

Bildarchiv Steffens/akg images

Khadijah (A.D. 556–A.D. 619), portrayed in a Turkish miniature, to the left of Gabriel and Muhammad

believed him immediately. She supported him as he preached his message and when others did not believe him, she encouraged to him to carry on. Khadijah was likely the first convert to Islam.

Muhammad loved Khadijah and he had no other wives while he was married to her. Many believe she was the love of his life and her death in 619 devastated Muhammad. She was buried in Mecca.

REVIEW & ASSESS

1. **Identify Main Idea and Details** Why did Khadijah hire Muhammad to help with her trading business?

_____

_____

2. **Make Inferences** Why do you think some people believed that Khadijah was the love of Muhammad's life?

_____

_____

UNIT 1 BIOGRAPHY
AL-ZAHRAWI

Al-Zahrawi was a scientist, a physician, a teacher, and a surgeon. His 30-volume encyclopedia influenced medical and surgical knowledge and procedures in medieval Europe. His work and observations provided the basis for many Western medical treatments for centuries.

- **Job:** Physician, Surgeon, Teacher
- **Major Work:** *Kitab al-Tasrif*
- **Home:** Andalusia, Spain

Al-Zahrawi, also known as Abul Kasim and Albucasis, was born in 936 in Córdoba, Spain. He was the court physician in Andalusia and the chief physician for the Umayyad Caliph al-Hakam II and the military ruler, al-Mansur. His medical career as a practitioner and teacher lasted more than five decades.

Al-Zahrawi's greatest contribution was his 30-volume, 1,500-page medical encyclopedia titled *Kitab al-Tasrif*, which means "The Method of Medicine." This illustrated encyclopedia built upon the earlier works of the ancient Greeks and Romans.

The *Tasrif* classified about 325 diseases and listed their symptoms and treatments. The volumes covered a stunning number of topics, including surgery, medicine, dentistry, nutrition, childbirth, elder care, orthopedics, and pharmacology. Al-Zahrawi also emphasized the importance of the doctor-patient relationship and was known to refer to his patients as his children.

The most influential of the volumes of the *Tasrif* was the 300-page volume that focused on surgery and surgical

Al-Zahrawi (936–1013) assisting a patient in a 1912 painting by Ernest Board

methods. It included drawings of more than 200 medical instruments and descriptions of how they could be used in surgery. Many of those instruments were invented by al-Zahrawi himself.

Al-Zahrawi's goal was for the *Tasrif* to act as a reference collection for medical students and practicing physicians. That goal was realized and even exceeded. The *Tasrif* was translated into Latin in the 1100s and then later into other European languages.

For 500 years, al-Zahrawi's work was the leading textbook on surgery in Europe. The oldest medical text in England, dated from the mid-1200s, is very similar to parts of the *Tasrif*. Most European authors of surgical texts into the 16th century relied on al-Zahrawi heavily in their own books. Al-Zahrawi's work continues to be considered an important medical reference today.

REVIEW & ASSESS

1. **Summarize** Who wrote the *Kitab al-Tasrif*, what did it contain, and what was its purpose?

_____

_____

2. **Draw Conclusions** Why is the *Tasrif* considered al-Zahrawi's greatest contribution?

_____

_____

UNIT 1 — CHAPTER 3 LESSON 1.4
The Qur'an and Hadith

DOCUMENT-BASED QUESTION

Use the questions here to help you analyze the sources and write your paragraph.

DOCUMENT ONE: from the Qur'an

1A According to this passage, why did God create diversity among people?

_____

_____

1B Constructed Response According to the Qur'an, who are the noblest human beings?

_____

_____

DOCUMENT TWO: from the Qur'an

2A What instruction did God give to human beings in this passage?

_____

_____

2B Constructed Response According to the Qur'an, why did Allah create a world of diversity?

_____

_____

DOCUMENT THREE: Hadith

3A Explain in your own words what a hadith is.

_____

_____

3B Constructed Response According to this hadith, what should Muslims do to be worthy of entering paradise on the Last Day?

_____

_____

SYNTHESIZE & WRITE

According to sacred Islamic writings, how should people behave?

Topic Sentence: _____

_____

Your Paragraph: _____

_____

_____

_____

_____

CHAPTER 4 SECTION 1
North Africa

NATIONAL
GEOGRAPHIC
LEARNING

READING AND NOTE-TAKING

**SYNTHESIZE VISUAL AND
TEXTUAL INFORMATION**

Read Section 1 and study the map in Lesson 1.2. Use the
textual and visual information from the section as well
as the map in Lesson 1.2 to answer the questions below.

1. What is the title of the map?

_____

_____

2. What do the red lines on the map represent?

_____

_____

3. What kind of trade goods came from the area of the Niger River?

_____

_____

4. What city did the Romans conquer with the help of Berbers?

_____

_____

5. Around which year were camels introduced in North Africa?

_____

_____

6. What is the meaning of the word "Sahara"?

_____

_____

7. About how many miles was it across the desert to get from Timbuktu to Fez in the north?

_____

_____

NATIONAL
GEOGRAPHIC
LEARNING

READING AND NOTE-TAKING

<u>SEQUENCE EVENTS</u> As you read Lessons 1.2 and 1.3, take notes on the main events in the development of the African slave trade.

Development of the Slave Trade in Africa

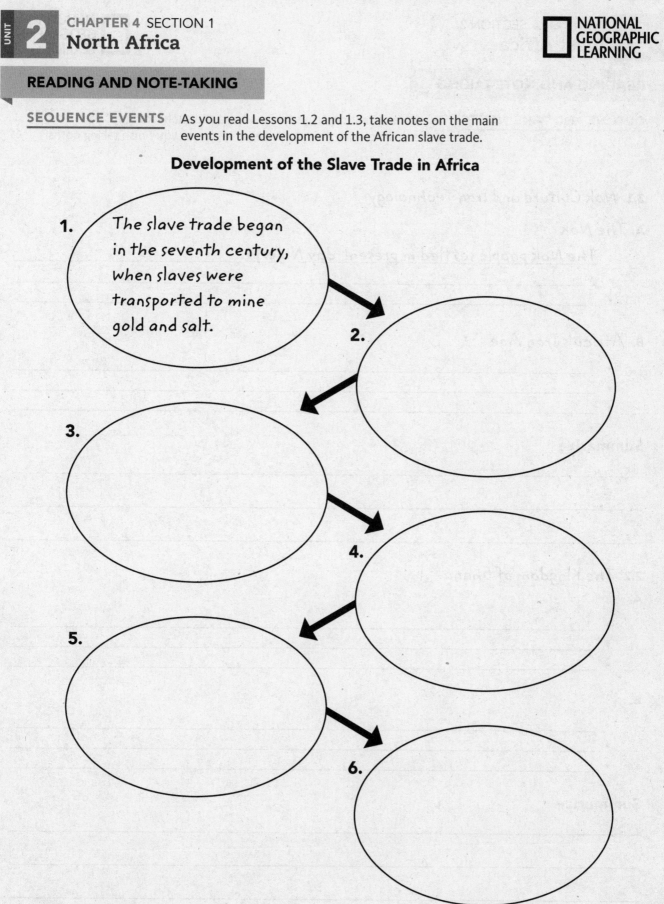

1. The slave trade began in the seventh century, when slaves were transported to mine gold and salt.

2.

3.

4.

5.

6.

Chapter 4 SECTION 1 **ACTIVITY B** WORLD HISTORY

UNIT **2**

CHAPTER 4 SECTION 2
West Africa

NATIONAL GEOGRAPHIC LEARNING

READING AND NOTE-TAKING

OUTLINE AND TAKE NOTES   As you read Section 2, use the headings and subheadings of each lesson to create an outline. Summarize each lesson as you finish taking notes.

2.1 Nok Culture and Iron Technology

A. The Nok

- The Nok people settled in present-day Nigeria. _____
- _____
- _____

B. Africa's Iron Age

- _____
- _____
- _____

Summarize

_____

_____

_____

2.2 The Kingdom of Ghana

A.

- _____
- _____
- _____

B.

- _____
- _____
- _____

Summarize

_____

_____

_____

2.3 The Empire of Mali

A.

- _____
- _____
- _____

B.

- _____
- _____
- _____

Summarize

_____

_____

_____

2.4 The Oral Tradition

A.

- _____
- _____
- _____

B.

- _____
- _____
- _____

Summarize

_____

_____

_____

UNIT 2 CHAPTER 4 SECTION 1
North Africa

NATIONAL GEOGRAPHIC LEARNING

VOCABULARY PRACTICE

KEY VOCABULARY

- **desertification** (dee-suhr-tih-fuh-KAY-shun) *n.* the process by which once fertile land is transformed into a desert

- **savanna** (suh-VAN-uh) *n.* an area of lush tropical grasslands

WDS TRIANGLES Complete Word-Definition-Sentence Triangles for the Key Vocabulary words *desertification* and *savanna*. Write the definition next to "D." Write a sentence using the word next to "S."

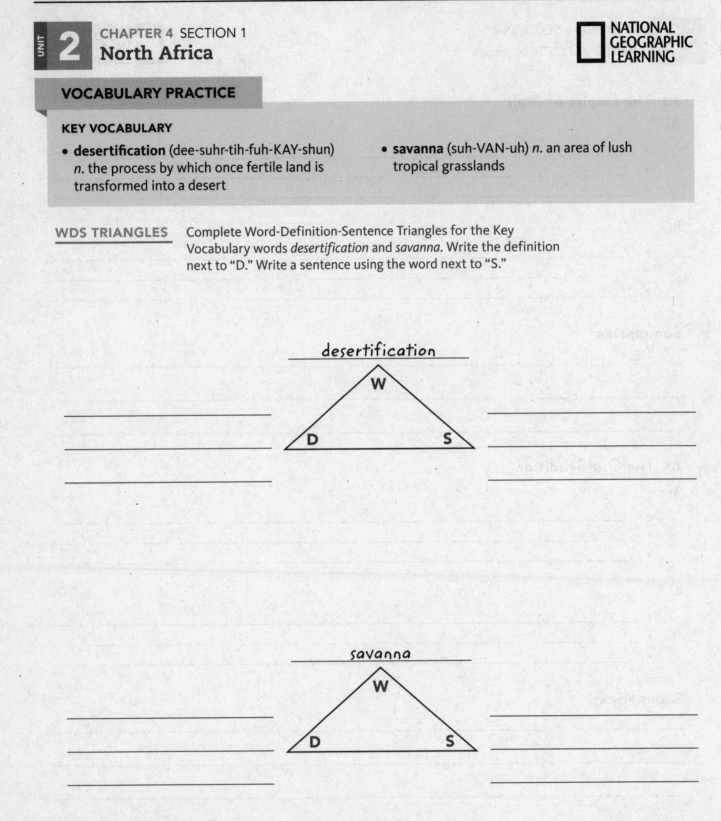

UNIT 2 CHAPTER 4 SECTION 1
North Africa

NATIONAL GEOGRAPHIC LEARNING

VOCABULARY PRACTICE

KEY VOCABULARY

- **caravan** (KAIR-uh-van) *n.* a group of people that travels together
- **commodity** (kuh-MAH-duh-tee) *n.* a trade good
- **scarcity** (SKAIR-suh-tee) *n.* a small supply of something
- **trans-Saharan** (trans-suh-HAHR-uhn) *adj.* across the Sahara

EXPOSITORY PARAGRAPH Write a paragraph that explains why people made great efforts to cross the Sahara to trade. Use the Key Vocabulary words *caravan*, *commodity*, *scarcity*, and *trans-Saharan* in your paragraph. Start with a strong topic sentence, and then write several sentences. Be sure to include a summary sentence at the end.

Topic Sentence:

_____

_____

_____

_____

_____

_____

_____

_____

_____

_____

_____

Summary Sentence:

_____

_____

_____

UNIT **2** **CHAPTER 4** SECTION 2
West Africa

NATIONAL GEOGRAPHIC LEARNING

VOCABULARY PRACTICE

KEY VOCABULARY

- **griot** (GREE-oh) *n.* a West African storyteller who relates stories through the oral tradition
- **oral tradition** *n.* the passage of spoken histories and stories from one generation to the next

COMPARISON CHART   Complete a Comparison Chart for the Key Vocabulary words *griot* and *oral tradition*. Write the definition and three details for each word. Then explain how the two words are related.

griot	oral tradition
_____	_____
_____	_____
_____	_____
_____	_____
_____	_____
_____	_____

How are the words related?
_____
_____
_____
_____
_____
_____
_____
_____

UNIT **2** **CHAPTER 4** SECTION 2
West Africa

VOCABULARY PRACTICE

KEY VOCABULARY

- **iron** *n.* a metal that is found in rock

- **mansa** (MAHN-sah) *n.* a West African king

- **terra cotta** (teh-ruh KAW-tuh) *n.* a fire-baked clay

UNIT 2 · CHAPTER 4 SECTION 2
West Africa

NATIONAL GEOGRAPHIC LEARNING

VOCABULARY PRACTICE

KEY VOCABULARY

- **iron** *n.* a metal that is found in rock
- **mansa** (MAHN-sah) *n.* a West African king
- **terra cotta** (teh-ruh KAW-tuh) *n.* a fire-baked clay

WORD SQUARE Complete a Word Square for the Key Vocabulary words *iron*, *mansa*, and *terra cotta*.

Definition	Characteristics
iron	
Examples	Non-Examples

Definition	Characteristics
Examples	Non-Examples

Definition	Characteristics
Examples	Non-Examples

Chapter 4 SECTION 2 **ACTIVITY B** WORLD HISTORY

Mali: Mansa Musa, King of Mali, holding a sceptre and a piece of gold. Detail from the Catalan Atlas, 1375 / Pictures From History/Bridgeman Images

UNIT **2**

BIOGRAPHY
MANSA MUSA

Mansa Musa ruled the West African kingdom of Mali at its height. He established control over trans-Saharan trade, making Mali one of the largest and wealthiest empires in the world.

- **Job:** King of Mali
- **Legacy:** Support of Education in Mali
- **Favorite Trip:** Pilgrimage to Mecca in 1324

Mansa Musa became the mansa, or king, of Mali in 1307. In 1324, Mansa Musa began his famous pilgrimage to Mecca, a journey of about 3,000 miles. Records by eyewitnesses reported that his caravan numbered 60,000 people, including 12,000 slaves wearing clothes made of fine silk. Eighty camels carried 300 pounds of gold each.

On the way to Mecca, Mansa Musa's caravan traveled east through North Africa. The caravan made news wherever it went. Upon arriving in Cairo, Egypt, Mansa Musa lavished so much gold throughout Cairo that the value of gold declined drastically.

Mansa Musa's journey to Mecca revealed the wealth of Mali. It also resulted in new trade routes and increased trade between Mali and Egypt. On his return, Mansa Musa brought back an Arabic library, religious scholars, and a Muslim architect. Mansa Musa commissioned the architect to build mosques and he oversaw the building of the Great Mosque of Timbuktu

One of Mansa Musa's greatest legacies was his support of education in his empire. He built schools, including the University of Sankore in Timbuktu, and he encouraged

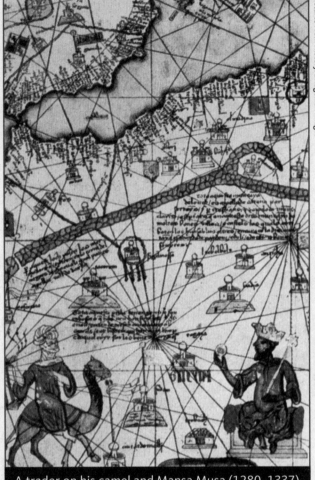

A trader on his camel and Mansa Musa (1280–1337), holding a nugget of gold in the *Catalan Atlas*

Muslim scholars to study in famous centers of learning around the world. During his rule, Timbuktu, already a center of trade, became the center of Islamic culture and learning. Scholars from all over the world came to Timbuktu to study.

The rulers who followed Mansa Musa after his death in 1337 were weak and unable to rule the huge empire as ably as he had. As a result, the Mali Empire declined and broke up into smaller kingdoms.

REVIEW & ASSESS

1. **Anazlye Cause and Effect** Why did Mansa Musa travel to Mecca and what effects did his journey have on Mali?

2. **Form and Support Opinions** What was Mansa Musa's most important achievement? Support your opinion with evidence from the reading.

_____

_____

CHAPTER 4 LESSON 2.5
Trans-Saharan Travelers

DOCUMENT-BASED QUESTION

Use the questions here to help you analyze the sources and write your paragraph.

DOCUMENT ONE: from Al-Umari's account of Mansa Musa's visit to Cairo in 1324

1A Why would Mansa Musa send the sultan a gift but then refuse the offer to meet him?

_____

_____

_____

1B Constructed Response What evidence from the text demonstrates that Mansa Musa was an immensely wealthy and religious man?

_____

_____

_____

DOCUMENT TWO: from the *Catalan Atlas*, c. 1375

2A How does this map differ from maps we use today?

_____

_____

_____

_____

2B Constructed Response Based on the map, what can you conclude about Mansa Musa's importance to West Africa?

_____

_____

_____

SYNTHESIZE & WRITE

How did Mansa Musa affect Mali and the rest of the world?

Topic Sentence: _____

_____

Your Paragraph: _____

_____

_____

_____

_____

_____

NATIONAL
GEOGRAPHIC
LEARNING

READING AND NOTE-TAKING

ANALYZE CAUSE AND EFFECT   As you read Lesson 1.1, complete a Cause-and-Effect Chart with the various factors that led to the decline of the prosperous trading kingdom, Aksum.

Decline
of
Aksum

UNIT **2** | **CHAPTER 5** SECTION 1
East Africa

**NATIONAL
GEOGRAPHIC
LEARNING**

READING AND NOTE-TAKING

<u>SEQUENCE EVENTS</u> As you read Lesson, 1.2, take notes on how Indian Ocean trade and a distinctive trading culture developed in East Africa.

Beginning: Traders stayed along the coasts when sailing from India to Arabia and Africa.

Describe How were dhows uniquely suited to travel in the Indian Ocean?

_____

_____

_____

UNIT **2**

CHAPTER 5 SECTION 2
Central and Southern Africa

READING AND NOTE-TAKING

SUMMARIZE   After you read Section 2, complete the boxes below with notes on the three cultures presented in Section 2. Add at least three details for each.

Bantu:

Great Zimbabwe:

Kongo:

UNIT **2**

CHAPTER 5 SECTION 2
Central and Southern Africa

READING AND NOTE-TAKING

SYNTHESIZE INFORMATION   Use the map and text in Lesson 2.1 to answer the questions below about the Bantu migrations. Then write a short paragraph to synthesize the information.

1. What does Bantu mean? To whom does "Bantu" refer? _____

_____

2. Where was the Bantu homeland? _____

_____

3. Who influenced the Bantu on the east coast of Africa? _____

_____

4. When did the Bantu migrations begin and end? _____

_____

5. To what part of Africa did the Bantu not go? Why? _____

_____

_____

6. Why were the Bantu successful in their new locations? _____

_____

_____

Summarize

_____

_____

_____

_____

_____

_____

UNIT 2 · CHAPTER 5 SECTION 1
East Africa

NATIONAL GEOGRAPHIC LEARNING

VOCABULARY PRACTICE

KEY VOCABULARY

- **dhow** (dow) *n.* a ship with a long, thin hull and triangular sails
- **mariner** (MAIR-ih-nuhr) *n.* a sailor
- **monsoon** (mahn-SOON) *n.* a strong seasonal wind in South and Southeast Asia
- **sultan** (SUHL-tuhn) *n.* a ruler of the Ottoman Empire

DEFINITION CHART Complete a Definition Chart for the Key Vocabulary words.

Word	Definition	Illustration	In Your Own Words
dhow			

UNIT
2

CHAPTER 5 SECTION 1
East Africa

NATIONAL GEOGRAPHIC LEARNING

VOCABULARY PRACTICE

KEY VOCABULARY

- **city-state** *n.* a city that controls the surrounding villages and towns
- **hub** *n.* a center

DEFINITION AND DETAILS CHART Complete a Definition and Details Chart for the Key Vocabulary words. For each word, write its definition and examples or other details related to the word from the section.

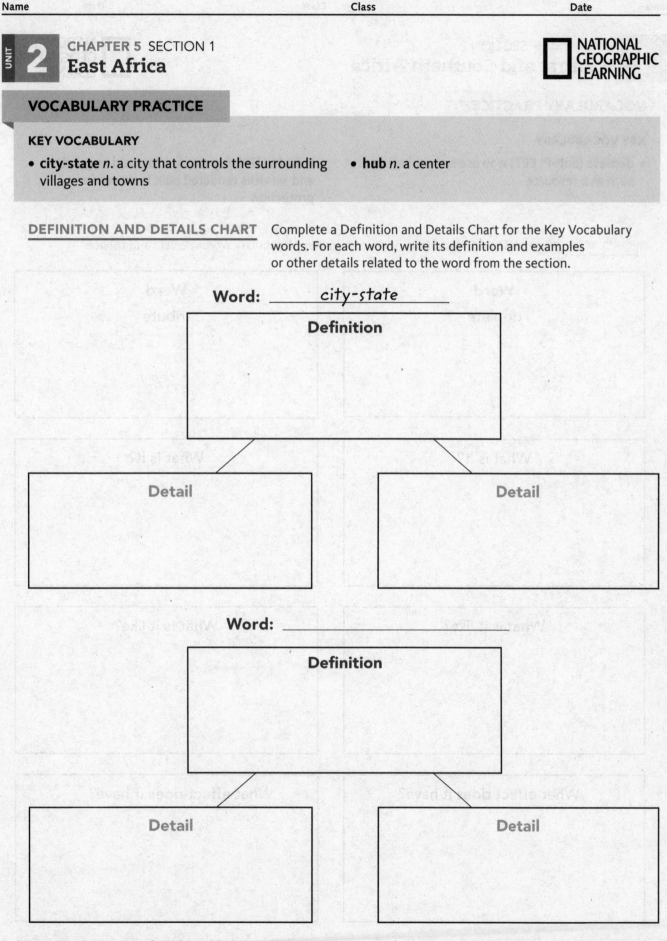

Word: _____ *city-state* _____

Definition

Detail

Detail

Word: _____

Definition

Detail

Detail

Chapter 5 SECTION 1 **ACTIVITY B** WORLD HISTORY

**NATIONAL
GEOGRAPHIC
LEARNING**

VOCABULARY PRACTICE

KEY VOCABULARY

- **deplete** (duh-PLEET) *v.* to use something up, such as a resource

- **tribute** (TRIHB-yoot) *n.* a tax paid or goods and services rendered paid in return for protection

WORD MAP Complete each Word Map below for the Key Vocabulary words *deplete* and *tribute*.

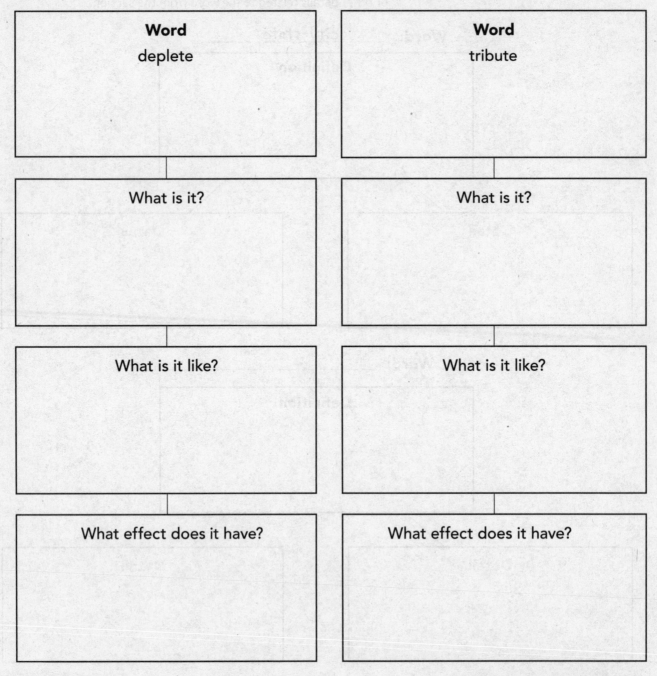

Word	**Word**
deplete	tribute

What is it?	What is it?

What is it like?	What is it like?

What effect does it have?	What effect does it have?

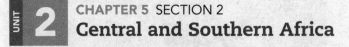

UNIT 2 — CHAPTER 5 SECTION 2
Central and Southern Africa

NATIONAL GEOGRAPHIC LEARNING

VOCABULARY PRACTICE

KEY VOCABULARY

- **lingua franca** (LING-gwuh FRAHNG-kuh) *n.* a language commonly used by many different groups of people

- **migration** (my-GRAY-shun) *n.* the movement from one place to another

Y-CHART Complete the Y-Chart below using the Key Vocabulary words *lingua franca* and *migration*.

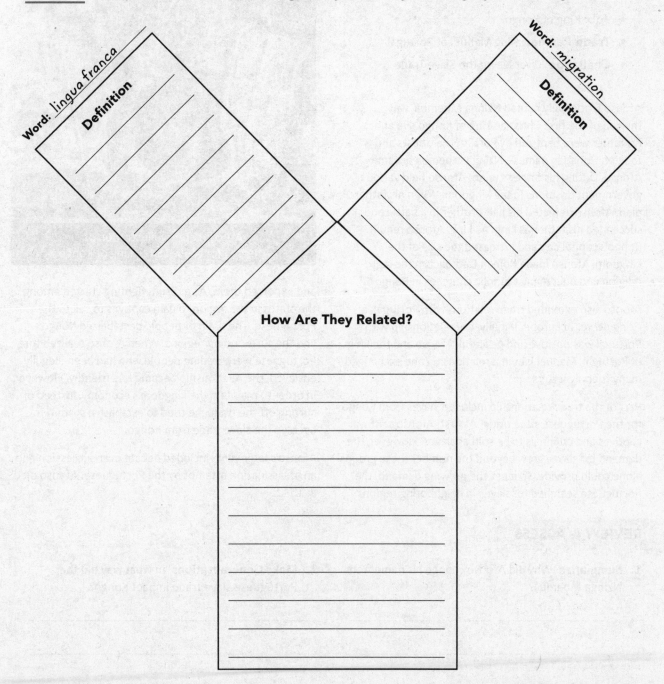

Word: *lingua franca*

Definition

Word: *migration*

Definition

How Are They Related?

Chapter 5 SECTION 2 **ACTIVITY B** WORLD HISTORY

UNIT 2

BIOGRAPHY

AFONSO I

Afonso I ruled the West African kingdom of Kongo in the 1500s. During his reign, he established a strong partnership with the European trading power, Portugal. This relationship impacted Kongo in dramatic ways.

- **Job:** King of Kongo
- **Trade Partner:** King Manuel of Portugal
- **Challenge:** Overseeing the Slave Trade

Afonso I, originally named Nzinga Mbemba, was the son of the first Christian king of Kongo. He and his father were baptized by Portuguese priests and took on Christian names—Nzinga Mbemba became Afonso. During his father's reign, Afonso held various government positions in the kingdom. When his father died, Afonso defeated his half-brother in a battle and succeeded his father as king. As king, Afonso rebuilt Kongo's capital city and increased the size of the kingdom. Afonso made Roman Catholicism the state religion and built many Catholic churches in Kongo.

Afonso also extended trade relations with Portugal, a rising power in Europe. Initially, the relationship with Portugal was positive and peaceful. Afonso and the king of Portugal, Manuel I, built a relationship and exchanged many friendly letters.

Part of the trade relationship included slaves from Kongo for the Portuguese slave trade. At first, Afonso sent war captives and criminals to be sold as slaves. However, the demand for slaves grew beyond the number these groups alone could provide. To meet the growing demand, the Portuguese searched for slaves in neighboring regions

A 17th-century illustration of Afonso I (c. 1460–1542), king of Kongo

and exported them. As a result, fighting started among the states in the region to gain captives to sell to the Portuguese. The drain of people destabilized Kongo and the surrounding regions. When Afonso realized the Portuguese were trading people who had been illegally enslaved, the relationship became less friendly. However, in order to maintain the kingdom's economy, instead of cutting off the trade, he tried to establish a system to oversee the slave trade from Kongo.

Afonso's later years included debate over succession and an assassination attempt by the Portuguese. Afonso died in 1542.

REVIEW & ASSESS

1. **Summarize** Why did Afonso change his name from Nzinga Mbemba?

_____

_____

2. **Make Generalizations** In what way did the Portuguese slave trade impact Kongo?

_____

_____

UNIT 3

CHAPTER 6 SECTION 1
The Olmec and the Zapotec

READING AND NOTE-TAKING

COMPARE AND CONTRAST   Complete a Y-Notes Chart to identify similarities and differences between the Olmec and the Zapotec.

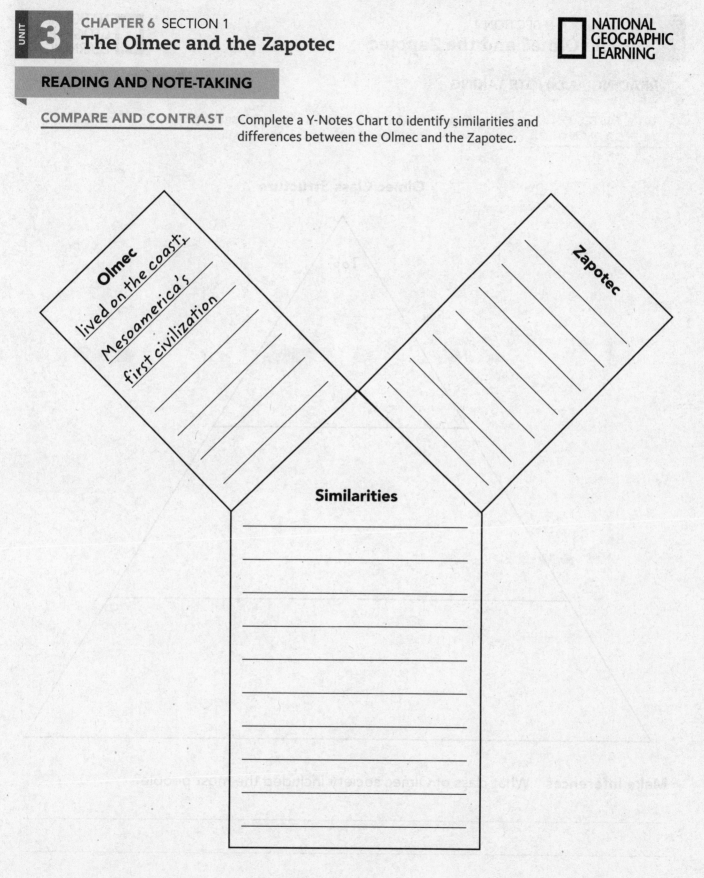

Olmec
lived on the coast;
Mesoamerica's
first civilization

Zapotec

Similarities

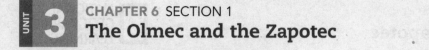

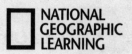

NATIONAL GEOGRAPHIC LEARNING

READING AND NOTE-TAKING

TAKE NOTES ON A TOPIC TRIANGLE   After reading Lesson 1.2, take notes in a Topic Triangle on the class structure of the Olmec. Then answer the question.

Olmec Class Structure

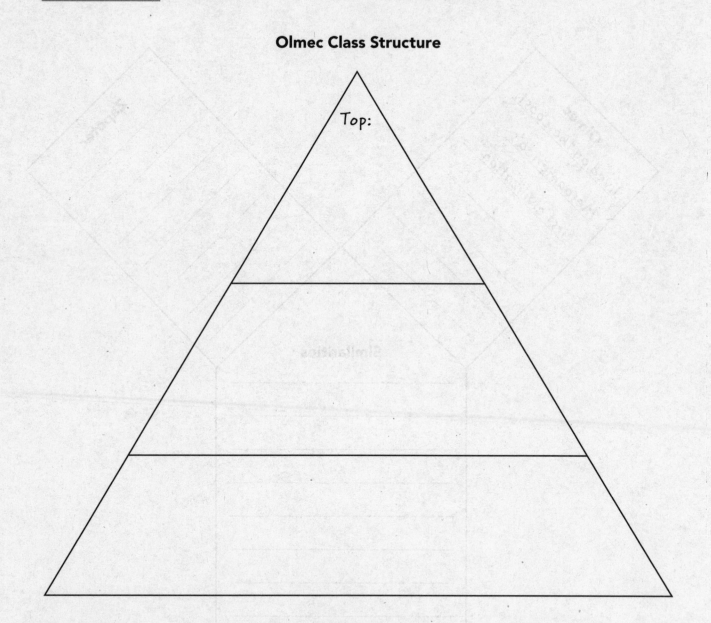

Top:

Make Inferences   What class of Olmec society included the most people?

_____

_____

_____

READING AND NOTE-TAKING

SEQUENCE EVENTS   As you read Section 2 take notes on a Sequence Chain
to track the development of Maya agriculture.

Maya's Agricultural Success

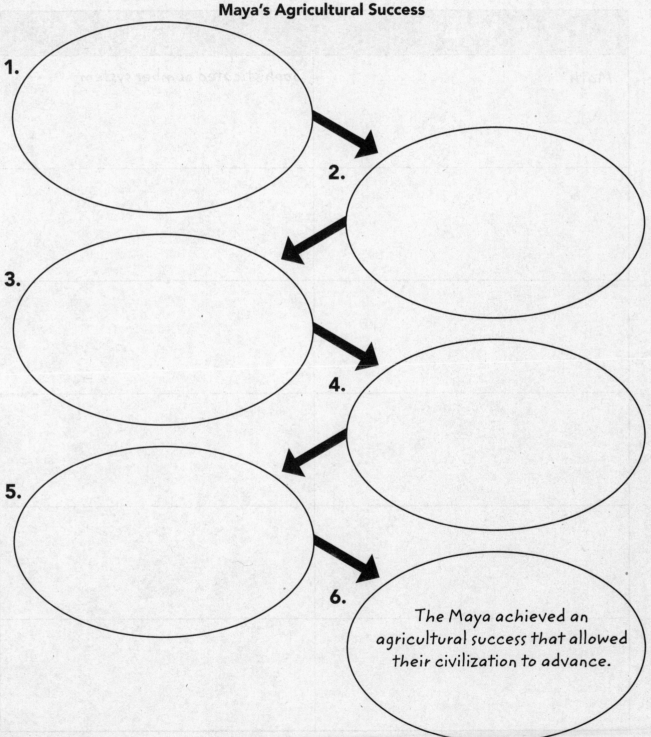

1.

2.

3.

4.

5.

6.

The Maya achieved an
agricultural success that allowed
their civilization to advance.

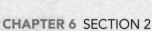

UNIT **3** CHAPTER 6 SECTION 2
The Maya

READING AND NOTE-TAKING

IDENTIFY LEGACIES   Use a chart to take notes on the different legacies left behind by the Maya as you read Lesson 2.4.

Subject	Legacy
Math	Sophisticated number system

Chapter 6 SECTION 2 **ACTIVITY B** **WORLD HISTORY**

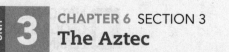

CHAPTER 6 SECTION 3
The Aztec

NATIONAL
GEOGRAPHIC
LEARNING

READING AND NOTE-TAKING

SYNTHESIZE VISUAL AND TEXTUAL INFORMATION

As you read Section 3 take note of the maps, photographs, and other visuals that will help you to synthesize the information you read. Then answer the questions below.

1. When did Aztec nomads move into the Valley of Mexico?

_____

_____

_____

2. What is the title of the map in Lesson 3.1?

_____

_____

_____

3. What was the Triple Alliance?

_____

_____

_____

_____

4. According to the map and the text in Lesson 3.1, what lake was the center of Aztec civilization?

_____

_____

_____

5. Who does the mask in Lesson 3.1 depict? What is the mask made of?

_____

_____

_____

NATIONAL
GEOGRAPHIC
LEARNING

6. What is the photograph in Lesson 3.2? What does it tell us about the Aztec?

_____

_____

_____

7. How would you describe Moctezuma II, based on the illustration and the text in Lesson 3.3?

_____

_____

_____

_____

8. Where and when did Hernán Cortés arrive in Aztec Empire? Why was he there?

_____

_____

_____

9. Based on your reading, why did some Aztec join Cortés and fight against their own leader?

_____

_____

_____

_____

10. How long did it take for the Spanish to overpower the city of Tenochtitlán?

_____

_____

_____

CHAPTER 6 SECTION 1
The Olmec and the Zapotec

NATIONAL GEOGRAPHIC LEARNING

VOCABULARY PRACTICE

KEY VOCABULARY

- **mother culture** *n.* a civilization that greatly influences other civilizations

- **terrace** (TEHR-uhs) *n.* a stepped platform built into a mountainside

WORD WEB Complete a Word Web for the Key Vocabulary words *mother culture* and *terrace*. Add information, ideas, and related words that help explain the meaning of each word.

Word: *mother culture*

Word: *terrace*

Definition

Definition

UNIT **3**

CHAPTER 6 SECTION 1
The Olmec and the Zapotec

NATIONAL GEOGRAPHIC LEARNING

VOCABULARY PRACTICE

KEY VOCABULARY

- **cacao** (kuh-COW) *n.* a bean used to make chocolate

- **highland** *n.* a type of land that is high above the sea

- **lowland** *n.* a type of land that is low and level

- **maize** (MAYZ) *n.* a type of corn first domesticated by early Mesoamericans

- **slash-and-burn agriculture** *n.* a method of clearing fields for planting

WRITE A SUMMARY   Reread Lesson 1.1. Then write a summary of the lesson using all five Key Vocabulary words. Underline the vocabulary words when they appear in your summary. Use the words in a way that defines and explains them.

UNIT 3 — CHAPTER 6 SECTION 2
The Maya

VOCABULARY PRACTICE

KEY VOCABULARY

- **codex** (KOH-decks) *n.* a folded book made of tree bark paper

- **glyph** (glihf) *n.* a symbolic picture used to represent a word, syllable, or sound

VOCABULARY T-CHART Use a T-Chart to compare the meanings of the Key Vocabulary words *codex* and *glyph*. Write each word's definition and then list details about each word based on what you have read in Section 2. Then answer the question.

Word: *codex*	Word: *glyph*
Definition:	Definition:
Details:	Details:

Compare What is one way the meanings of *codex* and *glyph* are related?

_____

_____

_____

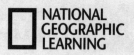

UNIT 3

CHAPTER 6 SECTION 2
The Maya

VOCABULARY PRACTICE

KEY VOCABULARY

• **creation story** *n.* an account that explains how the world began and how people came to exist

WORD WHEEL   Follow the instructions below to analyze the Key Vocabulary word.

1. Write the word in the center of the wheel.

2. Look in your textbook for examples of descriptions related to the word, or think of any related words you already know.

3. Write your descriptions and related words on the spokes of the wheel. Add more spokes if needed.

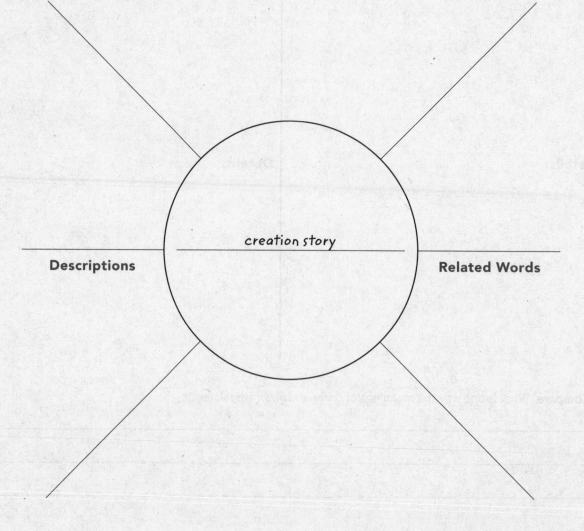

creation story

Descriptions   **Related Words**

UNIT 3
CHAPTER 6 SECTION 3
The Aztec

NATIONAL GEOGRAPHIC LEARNING

VOCABULARY PRACTICE

KEY VOCABULARY

- **chinampa** (chee-NAHM-pah) *n.* a floating field that supported agriculture
- **communal** (koh-MYOO-nuhl) *adj.* shared
- **conquistador** (kon-KEES-tuh-dohr) *n.* a Spanish conqueror who was looking for gold and other riches in the Americas

WORD SQUARE   Complete a Word Square for the Key Vocabulary words.

Definition	Characteristics
	chinampa
Examples	Non-Examples

Definition	Characteristics
Examples	Non-Examples

Definition	Characteristics
Examples	Non-Examples

UNIT 3

CHAPTER 6 SECTION 3
The Aztec

NATIONAL GEOGRAPHIC LEARNING

VOCABULARY PRACTICE

KEY VOCABULARY

- **noble** *n.* a member of a high class in society who inherits his or her status
- **serf** *n.* a person who lived and worked on the private land of a noble

TOPIC TRIANGLE   Use the Topic Triangle to help you understand the relationship between the Key Vocabulary words. Write three sentences about Aztec society, with the most general description in the top of the diagram and the most specific detail on the bottom level. Be sure that your diagram correctly uses both Key Vocabulary words.

Broad Topic

Narrow Topic

Quagga Media / Quagga Illustrations / Age Fotostock

UNIT 3 BIOGRAPHY
HERNÁN
CORTÉS

Hernán Cortés was a Spanish conquistador who conquered the Aztec Empire in 1521. Upon doing so, he claimed the empire's vast territory, which would remain part of Spain for the next 300 years.

- **Job:** Conquistador, Governor of New Spain
- **Childhood Hero:** Christopher Columbus
- **Home:** Spain

Hernán Cortés was born in 1485 to a prominent family in Medellín, a city in southwestern Spain. As a young man, he was intrigued by stories of Christopher Columbus's discoveries. Seeing ships returning with wealth and exotic goods settled the matter for Cortés: he would explore, too.

In 1504, Cortés sailed across the Atlantic to Hispaniola, then a Spanish headquarters. In 1511, under the leadership of Diego Velásquez, he helped make Cuba a Spanish colony. Spain also wanted to establish a colony on the North American mainland because of reports of a civilization that was rich in gold. Velásquez chose Cortés to start a colony there, too, in present-day Mexico. When he arrived in the Aztec Empire in 1519, Cortés sank his ships to prevent his men from leaving.

Many Aztec subjects hated their rulers and resented paying tribute to them. Cortés took advantage of the situation and made allies of more than 200,000 natives,

Portrait of Hernán Cortés (1485–1547)

called the Tlaxcalan. He marched into Tenochtitlán, the Aztec capital and the home of the emperor, Moctezuma II. Although Moctezuma received Cortés graciously, Cortés took him hostage and raided the city.

The Aztec drove the Spanish out of Tenochtitlán, but Cortés returned in 1521 with cannons and captured the city, effectively defeating the empire. The Spanish king was pleased with Cortés's victory and appointed him as the governor of New Spain in 1522. In 1540, Cortés returned to Spain. He died in 1547.

REVIEW & ASSESS

1. **Draw Conclusions** Why was Cortés able to make allies in the Aztec Empire?

_____

_____

2. **Make Generalizations** How would you describe Cortés's character?

_____

_____

© National Geographic Learning, Cengage Learning

UNIT 3

BIOGRAPHY
MOCTEZUMA II

Moctezuma II became the emperor of the Aztec, the most advanced civilization in North America, in 1502. He ruled the empire at its greatest height and extent.

- **Job:** Aztec Emperor
- **Education:** Aztec Warrior School
- **Enemy:** Hernán Cortés

Moctezuma II was born in 1466. After years of schooling and training in an Aztec warrior school, he earned a command in the army. In 1502, Moctezuma became the ninth Aztec emperor, succeeding his uncle. He ruled the Aztec for 20 years from the empire's capital city, Tenochtitlán, present-day Mexico City.

Moctezuma was a ruthless emperor who led a lavish lifestyle. He also led many campaigns that increased the size of his empire. Moctezuma's style of ruling created a number of enemies among the people he conquered. The Spanish conquistador Hernán Cortés used this discontent to his advantage when he and his soldiers invaded in 1519.

As was Aztec custom, Moctezuma welcomed Cortés with gifts of gold when Cortés arrived in Tenochtitlán. Cortés thought this hospitality was a trap and took Moctezuma hostage. Cortés believed that the Aztec would not attack the Spanish as long as he held their emperor captive. When Moctezuma was taken hostage, many Aztec lost respect for him. They believed he gave in to the Spanish too easily and had become weak.

The Spanish forced Moctezuma to order his subjects to end their resistance. In 1520, when Moctezuma tried

Portrait of Moctezuma II (1466–1520)

North Wind Picture Archives / Alamy

to address his people, the disgusted Aztec responded by throwing stones at him. Moctezuma was seriously wounded and died three days later. The Aztec and later historians claimed that the Spanish killed Moctezuma, though. Moctezuma's successors could not stop the Spanish from taking Tenochtitlán in 1521, and the Aztec Empire came to an end.

REVIEW & ASSESS

1. **Draw Conclusions** What kind of ruler was Moctezuma II?

_____

_____

2. **Summarize** How did the Aztec respond when Moctezuma was taken hostage?

_____

_____

UNIT 3 — CHAPTER 6 LESSON 2.5
Creation Stories

NATIONAL GEOGRAPHIC LEARNING

DOCUMENT-BASED QUESTION

Use the questions here to help you analyze the sources and write your paragraph.

DOCUMENT ONE: from the *Popol Vuh*

1A In this passage, to what is the rising of the Earth compared to?

_____

_____

1B Constructed Response According to this passage, how did the Maya gods form Earth?

_____

_____

DOCUMENT TWO: from the Book of Genesis

2A What action by God is described in the passage?

_____

_____

2B Constructed Response In this excerpt, what was the world like before God brought light to the earth?

_____

_____

DOCUMENT THREE: from *Pan Gu Creates Heaven and Earth*

3A How did Pan Gu break up the chaos into pieces?

_____

_____

3B Constructed Response In this myth, what elements formed heaven and what elements formed the earth?

_____

_____

SYNTHESIZE & WRITE

What are some common characteristics of creation stories?

Topic Sentence: _____

_____

Your Paragraph: _____

_____

_____

_____

CHAPTER 7 SECTION 1
Peruvian Cultures

READING AND NOTE-TAKING

CATEGORIZE INFORMATION Complete a concept cluster to group information about the Moche, Nasca, Wari, and Sicán cultures into categories.

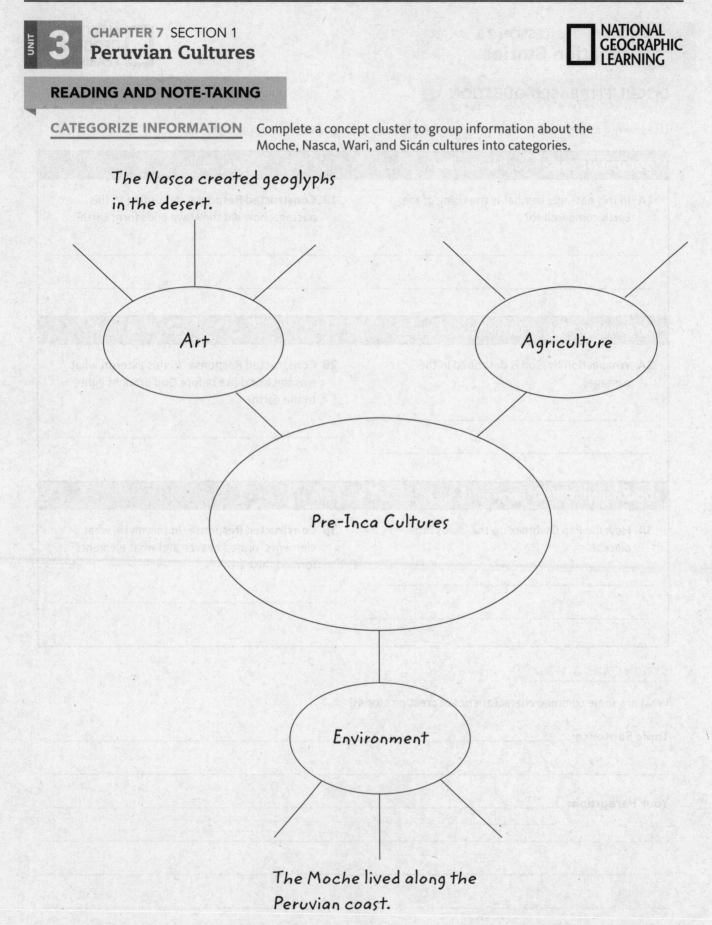

The Nasca created geoglyphs in the desert.

Art

Agriculture

Pre-Inca Cultures

Environment

The Moche lived along the Peruvian coast.

CHAPTER 7 SECTION 1
Peruvian Cultures

NATIONAL GEOGRAPHIC LEARNING

READING AND NOTE-TAKING

IDENTIFY PROBLEMS AND SOLUTIONS   Complete a Problem-and-Solution Chart to explain how Inca rulers managed an expansive territory and large population.

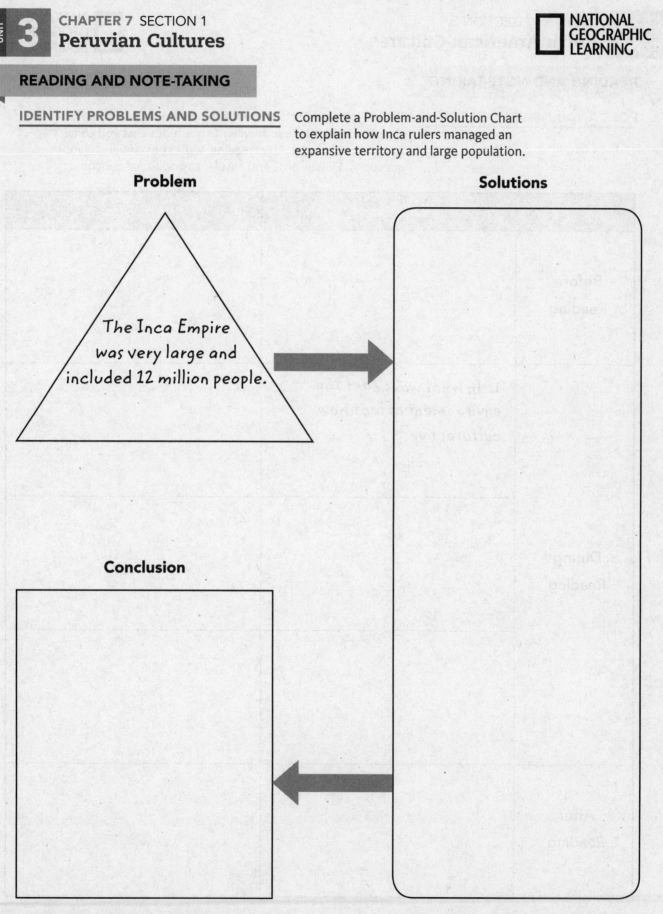

Problem

The Inca Empire was very large and included 12 million people.

Solutions

Conclusion

UNIT **3** CHAPTER 7 SECTION 2
North American Cultures

READING AND NOTE-TAKING

POSE AND ANSWER QUESTIONS Before you read Section 2, write a question in the Pose and Answer Questions chart below. Then write questions that you come to mind as you read. After reading, write the answers to your questions. Finally, pose and answer an additional question.

	Questions	Answers
Before Reading		
During Reading	1. In what ways does the environment affect how cultures live?	1.
	2.	2.
	3.	3.
After Reading		

UNIT 3
CHAPTER 7 SECTION 2
North American Cultures

READING AND NOTE-TAKING

<u>MAKE GENERALIZATIONS</u> Complete an Idea Diagram about the information in Lesson 2.3. Rewrite the introduction to the lesson in your own words. Then take notes on specific details under each subheading. After you finish reading, write a generalization about Great Plains cultures.

Lesson Title | Peoples of the Great Plains |

Introduction: _____
_____
_____

Subheading:
| Plains Dwellers |

Subheading:
| Buffalo Hunters |

Details:
_____   _____
_____   _____
_____   _____
_____   _____
_____   _____

Details:
_____   _____
_____   _____
_____   _____
_____   _____
_____   _____

Generalization: _____
_____
_____

NATIONAL GEOGRAPHIC LEARNING

UNIT 3

CHAPTER 7 SECTION 1
Peruvian Cultures

VOCABULARY PRACTICE

KEY VOCABULARY

- **geoglyph** (JEE-oh-glif) *n.* a large, geometric design or shape drawn on the ground

- **quarry** (KWAHR-ree) *v.* to extract something, such as stone, from the earth

WDS TRIANGLES Complete Word-Definition-Sentence Triangles for the Key Vocabulary words *geoglyph* and *quarry*. Write the definition next to "D." Write a sentence using the word next to "S." Write a sentence using the word next to "S."

geoglyph

W

D   S

_____   _____

_____   _____

_____   _____

_____   _____

quarry

W

D   S

_____   _____

_____   _____

_____   _____

_____   _____

VOCABULARY PRACTICE

KEY VOCABULARY

- **quinoa** (KEEN-wah) *n.* a high-protein grain native to the Andes Mountains in South America

- **terrace farming** *n.* a type of farming in which flat steps are cut into a mountain to provide farmland

VOCABULARY T-CHART   Use a T-Chart to compare the meanings of the Key Vocabulary words *quinoa* and *terrace farming*. Write the definition of each word and then write details about each word from what you know and what you have read. Then answer the question.

Word: *quinoa*	**Word:** *terrace farming*
Definition:	**Definition:**

Explain   What is one way the two Key Vocabulary words are related?

_____

_____

_____

UNIT 3 — CHAPTER 7 SECTION 2
North American Cultures

NATIONAL GEOGRAPHIC LEARNING

VOCABULARY PRACTICE

KEY VOCABULARY

- **adobe** (uh-DOH-bee) *n.* a kind of clay that when dried is used a a building material
- **confederation** (KUHN-fed-uhr-ay-shun) *n.* a group of allies
- **kiva** (KEE-vuh) *n.* a circular-shaped chamber built in the ground by the ancient Pueblo
- **mound builder** *n.* a Native American culture that built mounds and cities in the Mississippi River Valley region between 1000 B.C. and A.D. 500
- **wigwam** *n.* a domed tent used as housing by the Algonquin in North America

DEFINITION CHART   Complete a Definition Chart for the Key Vocabulary words.

Words	Definition	In Your Own Words	Illustration
adobe			

UNIT 3

CHAPTER 7 SECTION 2
North American Cultures

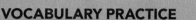
NATIONAL GEOGRAPHIC LEARNING

VOCABULARY PRACTICE

KEY VOCABULARY

- **potlatch** (PAHT-lach) *n.* a gift-giving ceremony practiced by the Kwakiutl and Haida Native American tribes

- **shaman** (SHAH-muhn) *n.* a medicine healer

- **totem pole** (TOH-tuhm) *n.* a tall, elaborately carved and painted tree trunk common in Northwest Coast native cultures

SUMMARY PARAGRAPH   Write a paragraph that describes Northwest Coast cultures. Use all of the Key Vocabulary words. Start with a strong topic sentence, and then write three to five sentences. Be sure to include a summary sentence at the end.

_____

_____

_____

_____

_____

_____

_____

_____

_____

_____

_____

_____

_____

_____

_____

_____

_____

_____

UNIT 3

BIOGRAPHY
PACHACUTI

The Inca emperor Pachacuti was known as the empire builder. His many accomplishments established the Inca Empire as one of the most powerful empires in the world.

- **Job:** Inca Emperor
- **Goal:** Unify and Expand Inca Empire
- **Name:** Means "He Who Changed the World"

Pachacuti became the Inca emperor in 1438. During his reign, he transformed a small kingdom into an Andean powerhouse by expanding territory, unifying different parts of the empire, and improving infrastructure. Historians sometimes compare Pachacuti to Philip II of Macedonia and Napoleon Bonaparte of France.

Pachacuti increased the size and reach of the Inca Empire through a number of military campaigns. He was able to conquer large parts of territory in the Urubamba Valley as well as the northwest coast of South America with little resistance because news had spread that becoming part of the Inca system brought prosperity. Once a territory was conquered, Pachacuti established laws that allowed his subjects to keep their traditional customs.

Throughout his reign, Pachacuti worked to unify the Inca Empire. He reorganized administrative offices and consolidated the Andean gods Inca subjects worshipped. He also expanded education and made Quechua the official language. Another way Pachacuti unified the Inca Empire was by developing a system of Inca runners called the *Chasqui*. These messengers ran from place to place to deliver communication all over the mountainous empire.

Statue of Pachacuti (1418–1471) in Cusco, Peru

In addition to unification, a main priority for Pachacuti was improving infrastructure. He rebuilt Cusco, the capital city, which included turning the course of two rivers so that they crossed the city and provided clean water. Pachacuti directed other building projects, too. He built an astronomical observatory and oversaw the building of bridges, temples, and palaces. Pachacuti also expanded the terrace farming system. Under his rule, villages built storehouses to put away food surpluses for future use. In 1450 he began construction of the city of Machu Picchu. Pachacuti ruled for more than 30 years and died in 1471.

REVIEW & ASSESS

1. **Draw Conclusions** Why was Pachacuti able to conquer such a large part of South America?

_____

_____

2. **Form and Support Opinions** What was Pachacuti's greatest accomplishment? Support your opinion with evidence from the reading.

_____

_____

UNIT 3

BIOGRAPHY

ATAHUALPA

Atahualpa was the last emperor of the Inca Empire, which at its height dominated much of the western part of South America. Atahualpa's capture and execution by Spanish conquistadors signaled the end of the empire.

- **Job:** Inca Emperor
- **Rival:** His Brother, Huáscar
- **Least Favorite Person:** Francisco Pizarro

Painting of Atahualpa (c. 1500–1533)

Atahualpa was favorite son of the Inca emperor named Huayna Capac. When Huayna Capac died in 1527, his sons divided the empire into two parts. Atahualpa ruled the northern part of the empire, and his brother, Huáscar, ruled the southern part.

The division of Inca Empire into separate parts led to a civil war. Atahualpa defeated and executed Huáscar along with his family. The civil war weakened the Inca. Important cities were destroyed and many people were killed. After defeating his brother, Atahualpa decided to rest in the small town of Cajamarca before going on to the capital of Cusco to take the throne. However, his plan soon changed. In 1531, the Spanish arrived in the Inca Empire. The Spanish conquistador named Francisco Pizarro had learned of the war between Atahualpa and his brother. He knew the instability caused by the civil war could work to his advantage.

In 1532, while Atahualpa was resting in Cajamarca, the Spanish conquistador Francisco Pizarro entered the town with 180 men. Pizarro invited Atahualpa to attend a feast. Seeing that the Spanish force was small, Atahualpa

accepted Pizarro's invitation. Atahualpa arrived the next day with several thousand unarmed followers. At the meeting, Pizarro demanded that Atahualpa convert to Christianity and accept the king of Spain as his ruler. When Atahualpa refused, armed Spaniards on horseback killed thousands of Inca and captured Atahualpa.

Hoping to be released, Atahualpa offered Pizarro a room filled with gold as ransom. Pizarro accepted the offer. Objects made of gold and silver were brought in from all over the empire. The Spanish forced the Inca to melt the items down, resulting in 24 tons of gold and silver to be sent to Spain. Once the Spanish had the riches, they executed Atahualpa. Atahualpa's death in 1533 marked the beginning of the end of the Inca Empire.

REVIEW & ASSESS

1. **Draw Conclusions** Why was Pizarro, with fewer than 200 men, able to defeat thousands of Atahualpa's men?

_____

_____

2. **Analyze Cause and Effect** What effect did giving gold and silver to the Spanish have on the Inca Empire?

_____

_____

UNIT 4

CHAPTER 8 SECTION 1
A Golden Age of Prosperity

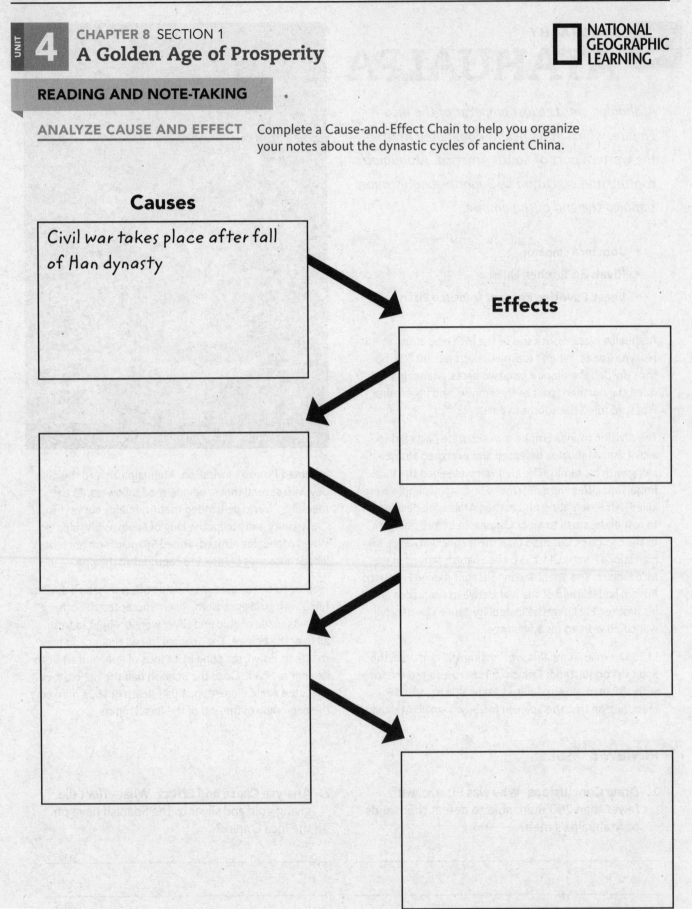

NATIONAL
GEOGRAPHIC
LEARNING

READING AND NOTE-TAKING

ANALYZE CAUSE AND EFFECT Complete a Cause-and-Effect Chain to help you organize your notes about the dynastic cycles of ancient China.

Causes

Civil war takes place after fall
of Han dynasty

Effects

READING AND NOTE-TAKING

IDENTIFY MAIN IDEA AND DETAILS Use a Main Idea and Details Web to organize your notes on technological advancements in ancient China.

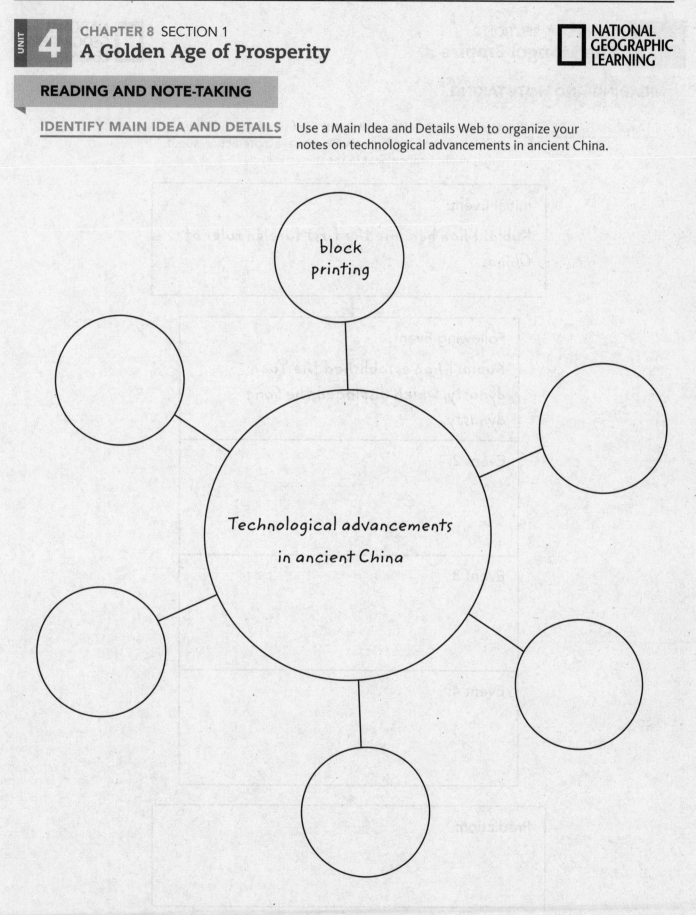

block printing

Technological advancements in ancient China

READING AND NOTE-TAKING

MAKE PREDICTIONS   Use the chart below to map out the events surrounding the fall of the Song Dynasty. Then make a prediction about what might happen next in the dynastic cycle.

> Initial Event:
>
> Kublai Khan became the first foreign ruler of China.

↓

> Following Event:
>
> Kublai Khan established the Yuan dynasty, which displaced the Song dynasty.
>
> Event 2:
>
> Event 3:
>
> Event 4:

↓

> Prediction:

UNIT **4**

CHAPTER 8 SECTION 2
The Mongol Empire

NATIONAL
GEOGRAPHIC
LEARNING

READING AND NOTE-TAKING

DRAW CONCLUSIONS   Use an Idea Diagram below to help you draw a conclusion about Chinese life during the Yuan dynasty. Be sure to include details under each main idea.

Topic: Chinese Life During the Yuan Dynasty

INTRODUCTION: _____

_____

_____

MAIN IDEAS:

| Literature flourished. | Peasants were treated poorly. | Merchants benefited from Mongol rule. |

DETAILS:

_____   _____   _____

_____   _____   _____

_____   _____   _____

_____   _____   _____

_____   _____   _____

CONCLUSION: _____

_____

_____

_____

NATIONAL GEOGRAPHIC LEARNING

UNIT **4**

CHAPTER 8 SECTION 3
The Ming Dynasty

READING AND NOTE-TAKING

SUMMARIZE ON DYNASTY MAPS   Use the Dynasty Maps below to summarize what you have learned about the Ming and Qing dynasties. Then write about the lasting effects that each dynasty had on Chinese culture and foreign policy.

Ming Dynasty (1368–1644)

Characteristics

1. Restored the Confucian values of the Tang and Song dynasties
2. _____
   _____
   _____
3. _____
   _____

Lasting Effects

_____
_____
_____
_____
_____
_____

Qing Dynasty (1644–1912)

Characteristics

1. _____
   _____
   _____
2. _____
   _____
   _____
3. _____
   _____

Lasting Effects

_____
_____
_____
_____
_____
_____

UNIT 4

CHAPTER 8 SECTION 3
The Ming Dynasty

NATIONAL GEOGRAPHIC LEARNING

READING AND NOTE-TAKING

SYNTHESIZE VISUAL AND TEXTUAL INFORMATION Use the chart below to record visual and textual information from Lesson 3.4 on bioarchaeology.

What is the title of the lesson? _____
What is the Main Idea? _____   _____   _____

What is the "Skeletal Secrets" passage about? _____ _____ _____ _____ _____	What is the "Puzzles from the Past" passage about? _____ _____ _____ _____ _____
What does the photograph above the lesson title show? _____ _____ _____ _____ _____	What is Christine Lee doing in the photograph? _____ _____ _____ _____ _____

Chapter 8 SECTION 3 **ACTIVITY B** WORLD HISTORY

UNIT 4 CHAPTER 8 SECTION 1
A Golden Age of Prosperity

NATIONAL GEOGRAPHIC LEARNING

VOCABULARY PRACTICE

KEY VOCABULARY

- **commerce** *n.* the buying and selling of goods
- **movable type** *n.* the individual clay tablets that could be arranged on a board to form text
- **porcelain** (POHR-suhl-uhn) *n.* a strong, light, and translucent ceramic
- **reunify** *v.* to join together again
- **staple** *n.* a main crop produced in a specific place

DEFINITION CLUES   Follow the instructions below for the Key Vocabulary word indicated.

1. Write the sentence in which the word *commerce* appears in Section 1.

_____

_____

_____

2. Write a definition of *movable type* using your own words.

_____

_____

_____

3. Use the word *porcelain* in a sentence of your own.

_____

_____

_____

4. What had to be done to *reunify* China?

_____

_____

_____

5. Write a sentence using *staple* and one other vocabulary word.

_____

_____

_____

UNIT 4

CHAPTER 8 SECTION 1
A Golden Age of Prosperity

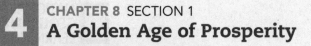
NATIONAL GEOGRAPHIC LEARNING

VOCABULARY PRACTICE

KEY VOCABULARY

- **nirvana** (nuhr-VAH-nah) *n.* in Buddhism, a state of bliss or the end of suffering caused by the cycle of rebirth

- **reincarnation** (ree-ihn-kahr-NAY-shuhn) *n.* in Hinduism, the rebirth of a person's soul into another body after death

COMPARISON CHART Complete a Comparison Chart below for both Key Vocabulary words. Write the definition and details for each word, and then explain how the two words are related.

nirvana	reincarnation
_____	_____
_____	_____
_____	_____
_____	_____
_____	_____

How are the words related?
_____
_____
_____
_____
_____
_____
_____

Chapter 8 SECTION 1 **ACTIVITY B** WORLD HISTORY

UNIT 4

CHAPTER 8 SECTION 2
The Mongol Empire

NATIONAL
GEOGRAPHIC
LEARNING

VOCABULARY PRACTICE

KEY VOCABULARY
- **khanate** (KAHN-ayte) *n.* a region of the Mongol empire
- **steppe** (STEP) *n.* a vast, grassy plain

DEFINITION CHART   Complete a Definition Chart for the Key Vocabulary words.

Word	khanate
Definition	
In Your Own Words	
Symbol or Diagram	

Word	steppe
Definition	
In Your Own Words	
Symbol or Diagram	

UNIT **4**

CHAPTER 8 SECTION 2
The Mongol Empire

NATIONAL GEOGRAPHIC LEARNING

VOCABULARY PRACTICE

KEY VOCABULARY

- **khanate** (KAHN-ayte) *n.* a region of the Mongol Empire
- **steppe** (STEP) *n.* a vast, grassy plain

DEFINITION CLUES   Follow the instructions for the Key Vocabulary word indicated.

VOCABULARY WORD: *khanate*

1. Write the sentence in which the word first appears in Section 2.

   _____

   _____

   _____

2. Write a definition using your own words.

   _____

   _____

   _____

   _____

3. Use the word in a sentence of your own.

   _____

   _____

   _____

   _____

4. Why do you think there were four khanates in the Mongol Empire?

   _____

   _____

   _____

   _____

VOCABULARY WORD: *steppe*

1. Write the sentence in which the word first appears in Section 2.

   _____

   _____

   _____

2. Write a definition using your own words.

   _____

   _____

   _____

   _____

3. Use the word in a sentence of your own.

   _____

   _____

   _____

   _____

4. Why do you think the Mongol tribes roamed across the steppes?

   _____

   _____

   _____

   _____

UNIT 4 · CHAPTER 8 SECTION 3
The Ming Dynasty

VOCABULARY PRACTICE

KEY VOCABULARY

- **isolationism** *n.* a rejection of foreign contact and outside influences

WORD MAP   Complete a Word Map for the Key Vocabulary word.

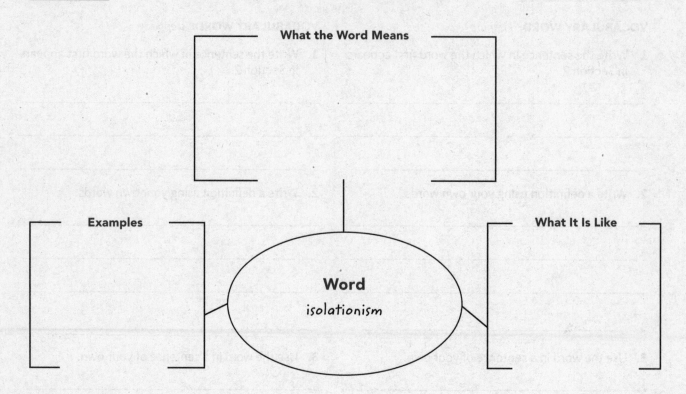

What the Word Means

Examples

What It Is Like

Word
isolationism

Make Connections What are some ways in which *isolationism* affects international relations? List examples.

_____   _____

_____   _____

_____   _____

_____   _____

UNIT 4

CHAPTER 8 SECTION 3
The Ming Dynasty

NATIONAL GEOGRAPHIC LEARNING

VOCABULARY PRACTICE

KEY VOCABULARY
- **isolationism** *n.* a rejection of foreign contact and outside influences

TRAVEL BROCHURE Create a travel brochure for visitors to the Great Wall of China. Draw a picture of the wall in the box below. Use the Key Vocabulary word in a paragraph that describes the site.

_____

_____

_____

_____

_____

_____

UNIT 4 BIOGRAPHY
KUBLAI
KHAN

Kublai Khan was brilliant warrior and an able statesman. Kublai completed the Mongols' conquest of China. He was a beloved ruler to both the Mongols and the Chinese.

- **Job:** Mongol Emperor
- **Founder:** Yuan Dynasty
- **Achievement:** Unified China

Kublai Khan was the grandson of Genghis Khan, the founder of the Mongol Empire. His father died when Kublai was 17, but Kublai did not get involved in empire affairs until he was in his thirties. In 1251, Kublai's brother, named Mngke, became the khan. Mngke gave Kublai control over Chinese territories in the eastern part of the empire. Kublai gathered a group of Chinese advisors to help him govern. Before Kublai, the Mongol approach was to destroy conquered territories and kill the people in them. Upon his advisors' suggestions, Kublai decided to rule differently and to treat the Chinese with respect.

In 1259, Mngke died in battle. Kublai became the next khan and founded the Yuan dynasty. During Kublai's rule, Mongols, who were the minority group, lived separately from the Chinese. Kublai accepted different religions in the empire, but granted privileges to the religious groups he favored. The Mongol Empire was divided into four social classes. At the top were the Mongols, followed by Central Asians and the northern Chinese. Southern Chinese made up the lowest social class. They were

Portrait of Kublai Khan (1215–1294)

Ancient Art & Architecture Collection Ltd / Alamy

barred from holding public offices and were used as laborers for public works.

Kublai Khan's missteps included costly wars and his extravagance, such as building luxurious palaces. These mistakes eventually drained the Chinese economy. After Kublai Khan's death in 1294, the Yuan dynasty gradually declined. Kublai's greatest achievement was unifying China, which had been divided since the 10th century A.D. Because of this achievement, Kublai Khan is considered one of China's great emperors and he is treated with respect by the Chinese.

REVIEW & ASSESS

1. **Draw Conclusions** Why is Kublai Khan considered one of China's great emperors?

_____

_____

2. **Analyze Cause and Effects** What caused the Yuan dynasty to decline?

_____

_____

UNIT 4 BIOGRAPHY
MARCO
POLO

Marco Polo was a Venetian merchant and an adventurer. His travels in China and other places are colorfully described in his book, The Travels of Marco Polo. *The accounts of his travels exposed Europeans to new places and inspired other adventurers to explore the world.*

- **Job:** Adventurer, Writer
- **Languages:** Italian, Turkish, Mongol
- **Home:** Italy, China, Italy Again

Marco Polo was born in Venice in 1254 to a family of merchants. Their Venetian trading business made them very wealthy. When Polo was about 17 years old, he and his father and uncle set out for China. They journeyed along the trade route known as the Silk Road through Persia and Afghanistan and across the Pamir Mountains into China. The Polos reached the Mongol court of Kublai Khan around 1275, where they lived for 17 years.

Marco Polo did not speak Chinese, but he did speak other languages, such as Turkish and Mongol. Kublai Khan liked Polo very much. He sent him on missions to distant places in the empire and enjoyed listening to the stories that Polo told when he returned. On the return trip from China to Venice, the Polos traveled by sea. They left with a caravan of several hundred people. The journey proved difficult, and many people died.

Soon after his return to Venice, Polo was captured by the Genoese, who were Venetian rivals, and imprisoned

Italian mosaic of Marco Polo (1254–1324)

in Genoa. While there, Polo met a fellow prisoner who was a famous writer. Polo dictated stories of his 25 years of travel to him, and the stories became the book *The Travels of Marco Polo.* The book made Marco Polo a celebrity. It was translated in French, Italian, and Latin and became the most popular book in Europe.

Because it included far-fetched and amazing stories, many people thought it was pure fiction. *Travels* eventually earned the title *Il Milione,* or "The Million Lies." On his deathbed, friends and family asked if what he had written in his book was true. Polo replied that he had not told half of what he had seen. Marco Polo died in Venice in 1324.

REVIEW & ASSESS

1. **Make Inferences** Why do you think Marco Polo's book became so popular in Europe?

_____

_____

2. **Form and Support Opinions** Do you think everything in Marco Polo's book was true? Support your opinion with evidence from the reading.

_____

_____

Travels on the Silk Roads

NATIONAL GEOGRAPHIC LEARNING

DOCUMENT-BASED QUESTION

Use the questions here to help you analyze the sources and write your paragraph.

DOCUMENT ONE: from *Genghis Khan and the Making of the Modern World*

1A What basic comparison is being made in this passage?

_____

_____

1B Constructed Response Why might the people living on the steppes benefit from Genghis Khan's rerouting of exports through their territory?

_____

DOCUMENT TWO: from *Travels* by Marco Polo

2A Explain how trade in Mongol China took place.

_____

_____

2B Constructed Response Why would using experts to determine prices make trade fairer and easier?

_____

DOCUMENT THREE: Passport Medallion, c. 1300

3A Why did the medallion have value beyond its physical worth?

_____

_____

3B Constructed Response How might Marco Polo have helped expand China's foreign contact and trade during the Mongol Empire?

_____

SYNTHESIZE & WRITE

During the Mongol Empire, how did Genghis Khan and Kublai Khan promote and increase trade?

Topic Sentence: _____

_____

Your Paragraph: _____

_____

_____

UNIT 4

CHAPTER 9 SECTION 1
Early Japan

NATIONAL GEOGRAPHIC LEARNING

READING AND NOTE-TAKING

SEQUENCE EVENTS   In the Sequence Chain below, list the major events addressed in Section 1. Start your Sequence Chain with the Jomon people and end with the establishment of the Japanese constitution.

Early Japan

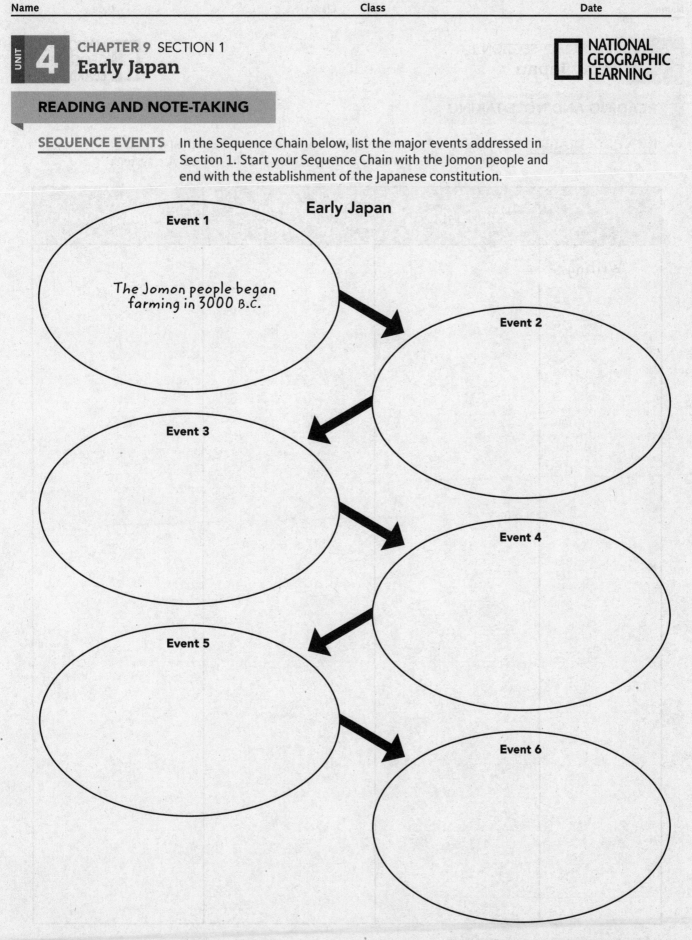

Event 1

The Jomon people began farming in 3000 B.C.

Event 2

Event 3

Event 4

Event 5

Event 6

UNIT **4** CHAPTER 9 SECTION 1
Early Japan

NATIONAL
GEOGRAPHIC
LEARNING

READING AND NOTE-TAKING

IDENTIFY STRATEGIES   Complete a Problem-and-Solution Table to show how the Japanese adapted Chinese ideas regarding writing and the civil service system.

Idea	Chinese Form	Problem Posed for Japanese	Japanese Solution
Writing			

UNIT 4

CHAPTER 9 SECTION 2
Japanese Art and Culture

NATIONAL GEOGRAPHIC LEARNING

READING AND NOTE-TAKING

ANALYZE PRIMARY SOURCES   Use the Idea Diagram below to analyze the primary sources in Lesson 2.2. For each source, record the document type and title, the main idea, and two observations about each document.

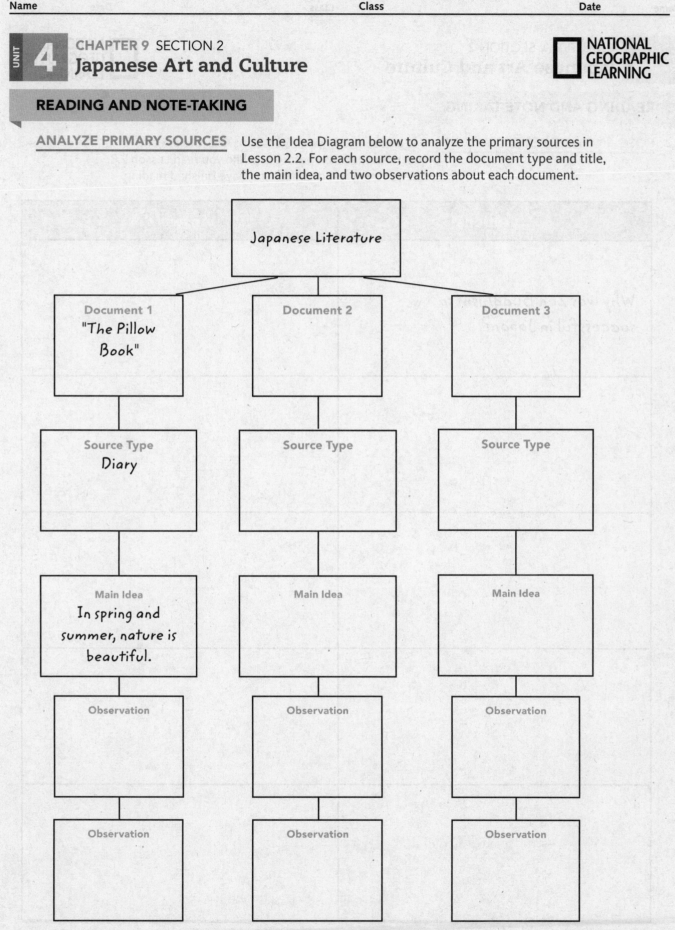

Japanese Literature

Document 1	Document 2	Document 3
"The Pillow Book"		

Source Type	Source Type	Source Type
Diary		

Main Idea	Main Idea	Main Idea
In spring and summer, nature is beautiful.		

Observation	Observation	Observation

Observation	Observation	Observation

UNIT 4 **CHAPTER 9** SECTION 2
Japanese Art and Culture

READING AND NOTE-TAKING

POSE AND ANSWER QUESTIONS Use a Pose and Answer Questions Chart to ask any questions that arise before or while you read Lesson 2.3. Answer the questions after you have finished reading.

Questions	Answers
Why was Zen Buddhism so successful in Japan?	

UNIT 4

CHAPTER 9 SECTION 3
Japanese Feudalism

NATIONAL
GEOGRAPHIC
LEARNING

READING AND NOTE-TAKING

OUTLINE AND TAKE NOTES   Complete an outline to help organize your notes on Section 3.

Topic: *Feudalism*

1. Under feudalism people were ranked in this way: symbolic emperor, shogun, daimyos, vassal samurai, peasants.

2. _____

_____

3. _____

_____

Topic: *Samurai*

1. _____

_____

2. _____

_____

3. _____

_____

Topic: *Warrior Culture*

1. _____

_____

2. _____

_____

3. _____

_____

CHAPTER 9 SECTION 3
Japanese Feudalism

Topic: Mongol Invasion

1. _____
   _____

2. _____
   _____

3. _____
   _____

Topic: Tokugawa Ieyasu

1. _____
   _____

2. _____
   _____

3. _____
   _____

Topic: Japanese Isolationism

1. _____
   _____

2. _____
   _____

3. _____
   _____

UNIT 4
CHAPTER 9 SECTION 1
Early Japan

NATIONAL GEOGRAPHIC LEARNING

VOCABULARY PRACTICE

KEY VOCABULARY

- **archipelago** (AHR-kuh-peh-luh-goh) *n.* a collection of islands

- **embassy** (EMH-bah-see) *n.* a group of people who represent their nation in a foreign country

- **regent** (REE-jehnt) *n.* a person who rules when a monarch or emperor is unable to do so

- **ritual** *n.* a formal series of acts always performed in the same way; a religious ceremony

WDS CHART Complete a Word-Definition-Sentence (WDS) Chart for each Key Vocabulary word.

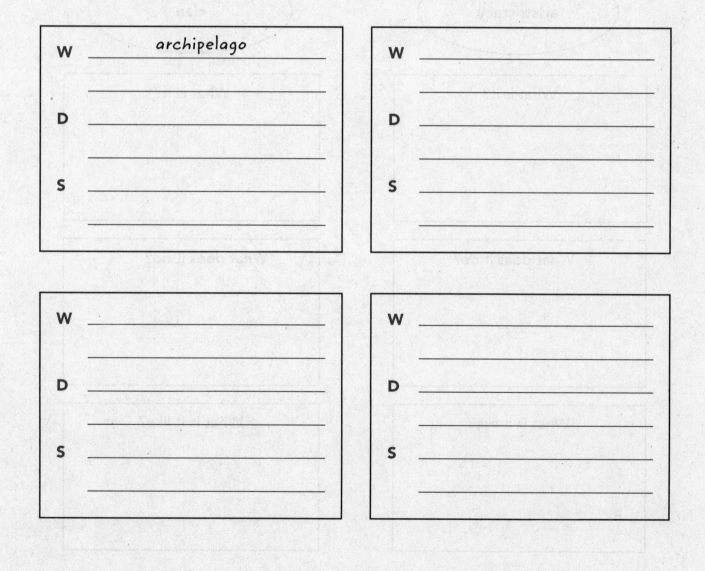

W ____ *archipelago* ____

D _____

S _____

W _____

D _____

S _____

W _____

D _____

S _____

W _____

D _____

S _____

UNIT 4

CHAPTER 9 SECTION 1
Early Japan

NATIONAL GEOGRAPHIC LEARNING

VOCABULARY PRACTICE

KEY VOCABULARY

- **aristocracy** (air-ih-STOCK-ruh-see) *n.* an upper class that is richer and more powerful than the rest of society

- **clan** *n.* a group of families that shares a common ancestor

WORD MAPS   Complete Word Maps for the Key Vocabulary words *aristocracy* and *clan*.

aristocracy

What is it?

What does it do?

What is it like?

clan

What is it?

What does it do?

What is it like?

CHAPTER 9 SECTION 2
Japanese Art and Culture

NATIONAL GEOGRAPHIC LEARNING

VOCABULARY PRACTICE

KEY VOCABULARY

- **kabuki** (kuh-BOO-kee) *n.* a form of Japanese drama that involves luxurious costumes and elaborate makeup

- **noh** (noh) *n.* a form of drama that grew out of Shinto rituals and often retells well-known folktales

VENN DIAGRAM Complete a Venn Diagram to compare and contrast the meanings of the Key Vocabulary words *kabuki* and *noh*.

kabuki   noh

Describe What functions did kabuki and noh serve in medieval Japan?

_____

_____

UNIT **4**

CHAPTER 9 SECTION 2
Japanese Art and Culture

NATIONAL GEOGRAPHIC LEARNING

VOCABULARY PRACTICE

KEY VOCABULARY

• **haiku** (HY-koo) *n.* a form of poetry that has 17 syllables in three unrhymed lines of 5, 7, and 5 syllables

• **meditation** (meh-duh-TAY-shun) *n.* the act of achieving inner peace and an enlightened realization of the divine aspect in each person

MEANING MAP Complete a Meaning Map for each Key Vocabulary word. Then answer the question.

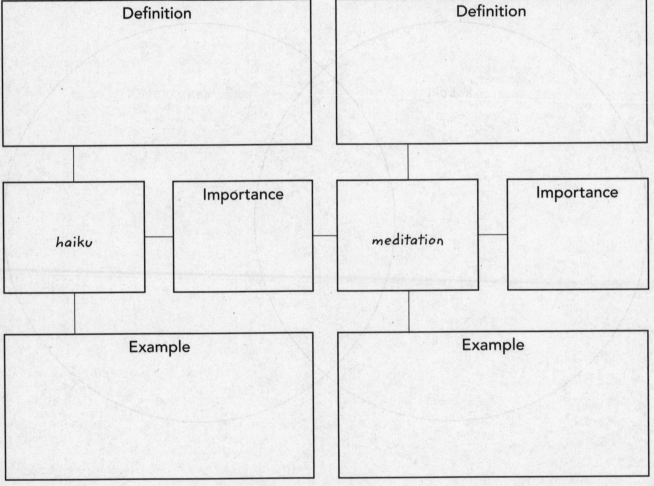

Definition

Definition

Importance

haiku

Importance

meditation

Example

Example

Summarize Write a sentence that describes the purpose of haiku and meditation in Japanese culture.

_____

_____

Chapter 9 SECTION 2 **ACTIVITY B** WORLD HISTORY

4 CHAPTER 9 SECTION 3
Japanese Feudalism

UNIT

NATIONAL GEOGRAPHIC LEARNING

VOCABULARY PRACTICE

KEY VOCABULARY

- **daimyo** (DY-mee-oh) *n.* a class of large landowning families in medieval Japan

- **feudalism** (FYOOD-ah-lih-zuhm) *n.* a political and social system in which a vassal receives protection from a lord in exchange for obedience and service

- **samurai** (SAM-uh-ry) *n.* a hired warrior in medieval Japan

- **vassal** (VASS-uhl) *n.* a person, usually a lesser nobleman, who received land and protection from a feudal lord in exchange for obedience and service

DESCRIPTIVE PARAGRAPH   Write a paragraph describing the structure of Japanese society using the Key Vocabulary words. Write a clear topic sentence as your first sentence. Then write several sentences with supporting details. Conclude your paragraph with a summarizing sentence.

Topic Sentence: _____

_____

_____

_____

_____

_____

_____

_____

_____

_____

_____

_____

_____

_____

_____

Summary Sentence: _____

_____

_____

UNIT 4 — CHAPTER 9 SECTION 3
Japanese Feudalism

NATIONAL GEOGRAPHIC LEARNING

VOCABULARY PRACTICE

KEY VOCABULARY

- **bushido** (BUSH-ih-doh) *n.* a strict code of behavior followed by the samurai in feudal Japan
- **shogun** (SHOH-guhn) *n.* the military ruler of medieval Japan
- **shogunate** (SHO-guhn-ate) *n.* the rule by a shogun

TOPIC TRIANGLE Use a Topic Triangle to help you understand the relationship between the Key Vocabulary words. Write three sentences about Japan's military rule, with the most general description on the top of the diagram and the most specific detail on the bottom level. Be sure that your diagram correctly uses all three Key Vocabulary words.

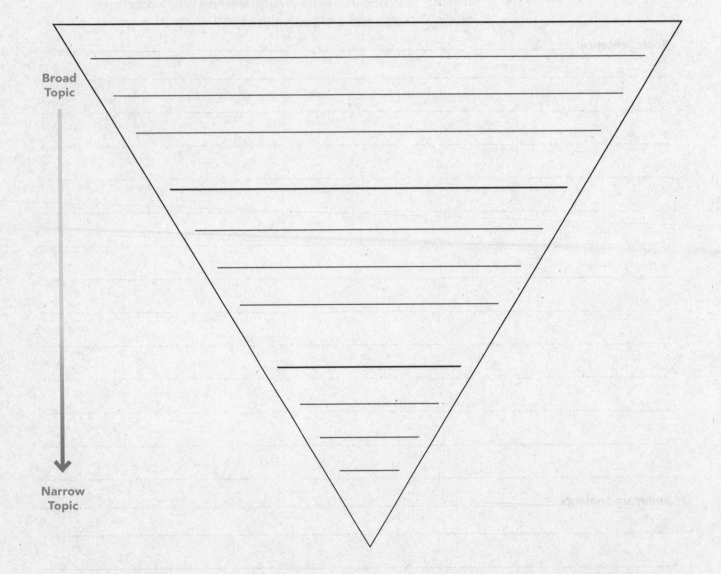

Broad Topic

Narrow Topic

UNIT 4 BIOGRAPHY
PRINCE SHOTOKU

Prince Shotoku served as the regent of Japan from 593 until his death in 622. He reshaped the Japanese government and brought Confucian ideas and Buddhism to Japan.

- **Job:** Crown Prince and Regent
- **Goal:** Improving Relations with China
- **Influences:** Confucianism and Buddhism

Born in Yamato, Japan, in 574, Prince Shotoku was a member of the powerful Soga family. After the death of his father, Shotoku's aunt became empress. Shotoku was named crown prince and regent, making him the effective ruler of the country.

As regent, Shotoku was able to re-open cultural and political channels with China. Chinese culture greatly impressed Shotoku—so much so that he introduced many Chinese ideas to Japan. He sent representatives to China and brought back hundreds of scholars, artists, and craftsmen.

Shotoku reshaped the Japanese government by incorporating many Chinese influences, which included setting up a centralized government and bureaucracy. In 604, Shotoku introduced the Seventeen Article Constitution. This code of laws for the ruling class stressed obedience to the emperor and the duty of the emperor to take care of his subjects. Shotoku stressed the Confucian idea of establishing a united country ruled by one person. He divided government positions into ranks that were recognizable by the color of the

Statue of Prince Shotoku (574–622)

headgear that people wore. Doing so allowed positions to be awarded based on merit rather than on heredity.

Prince Shotoku was also influenced by Chinese religious practices and during his reign he introduced Buddhism to Japan. He promoted Buddhism by building temples throughout the country. In time, Buddhism became integrated with Japanese Shinto traditions. Shotoku died in Yamato, Japan, in 622. After he died, he was considered a Buddhist saint.

REVIEW & ASSESS

1. **Summarize** In what ways did Chinese culture influence Prince Shotoku?

   _____

   _____

2. **Make Inferences** How do you think bringing Chinese scholars, artists, and craftsmen into Japan affected Japanese culture?

   _____

   _____

UNIT 4

BIOGRAPHY
MURASAKI SHIKIBU

Murasaki Shikibu wrote one of the greatest pieces of Japanese literature, The Tale of Genji. *Her book continues to be highly regarded, and it is the world's oldest novel.*

- **Job:** Poet, Novelist
- **Hobby:** Journal Writing
- **Major Works:** *The Tale of Genji, The Diary of Lady Murasaki, Poetic Memoirs*

Murasaki Shikibu was born in Kyoto, Japan, around 973. She was brilliant, and her father, a famous scholar, allowed her to study with her brother. At that time, being educated with males was considered improper for females. Shikibu married in her twenties and had one child, a daughter.

Shikibu's husband died in 1001, at which point the imperial family, who knew about her writing talents, brought her to the court. Shikibu pleased the empress and her court with the beautiful verses that she wrote.

Soon after arriving at the imperial court, Shikibu started a journal in which she recorded vivid descriptions of life at court. Shikibu used her journal entries as a resource when writing *The Tale of Genji*. This novel tells the story of a fictitious prince, Genji, and his romances. Shikibu's writing explores many human emotions. It also demonstrates her intimate understanding of aristocratic and court life, as well as her love of nature and her vast knowledge in many subjects. *The Tale of Genji*, which was meant to be read aloud, became

A kakemono, or hanging silk scroll, portraying Murasaki Shikibu (973–1025)

popular as soon as it was released. The manuscript was translated into several languages.

Shikibu continued her writing after she left the court. Some of her later works suggest that she anticipated the dramatic changes that were coming to the extravagant life of the upper class. Shikibu died around 1025 in Kyoto. Hundreds of years later, *The Tale of Genji* continues to fascinate readers. In 1935, Arthur Waley wrote what is considered the best-known English translation. A second English translation was published in 1976 and a third in 2001.

REVIEW & ASSESS

1. **Draw Conclusions** Why was Murasaki Shikibu asked to join the imperial family in their court?

_____

_____

2. **Make Inferences** How was the upbringing of Murasaki Shikibu not typical for women in 10th-century Japan?

_____

_____

UNIT 4

CHAPTER 9 LESSON 2.2
Poetry and Prose

NATIONAL
GEOGRAPHIC
LEARNING

DOCUMENT-BASED QUESTION

Use the questions here to help you analyze the sources and write your paragraph.

DOCUMENT ONE: from *The Pillow Book* by Sei Shonagon

1A What colors does Sei Shonagon use to describe the dawn in the spring?

_____

_____

1B Constructed Response Which parts of the day does Sei Shonagon find most beautiful in the spring and summer seasons? Why?

_____

DOCUMENT TWO: from *The Tale of Genji*

2A How is the poem spoken by Genji different from most other poems?

_____

_____

2B Constructed Response How does the writer use images of nature to express Genji's feelings?

_____

DOCUMENT THREE: Haiku by Matsuo Basho

3A Do you find this haiku appealing? Why or why not?

_____

_____

3B Constructed Response What feelings about nature does this haiku express?

_____

SYNTHESIZE & WRITE

What can you infer about early Japanese authors' relationship to nature?

Topic Sentence: _____

_____

Your Paragraph: _____

_____

_____

_____

UNIT 4

CHAPTER 10 SECTION 1
Korea's Early History

READING AND NOTE-TAKING

COMPARE AND CONTRAST   After reading Lesson 1.1, complete a Concept Cluster to help you categorize the characteristics of the different kingdoms of Korea. Add extra spokes to your Concept Cluster if necessary.

Silla

Koguryo

Three Kingdoms
of Korea

Paekche

UNIT 4

CHAPTER 10 SECTION 1
Korea's Early History

READING AND NOTE-TAKING

<u>SUMMARIZE GOALS AND OUTCOMES</u>   As you read Section 1, record details about Korea's early history on a Goal-and-Outcomes Chart. Then write a short summary about the details you chart.

Korea's Early History

Goals	Obstacles	Outcome
To be free of outside control	China's large area, strong government, and closeness to Korea	

Summary

UNIT 4

CHAPTER 10 SECTION 2
South and Southeast Asia

READING AND NOTE-TAKING

SUMMARIZE ON A CIVILIZATION MAP   As you read Section 2 on India, Vietnam, and Cambodia, complete Civilization Maps for the Gupta Empire, Dai Viet, and the Khmer Empire.

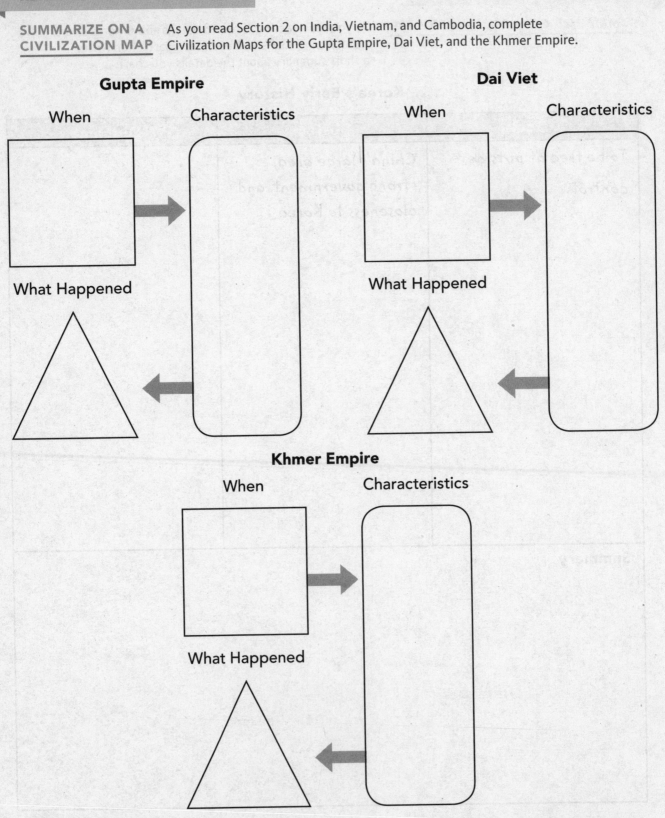

UNIT 4 CHAPTER 10 SECTION 2
South and Southeast Asia

READING AND NOTE-TAKING

CATEGORIZE RELIGIONS Keep track of details about Hinduism, Buddhism, and Islam as you read Section 2. Read each sentence below and decide which religion it applies to. On the line to the left of the sentence, write in **H, B,** or **I.**

_____ This religion has many gods and goddesses that are representations of a universal spirit called Brahman.

_____ This religion changed over time to include the worship of bodhisattvas, or enlightened beings.

_____ Angkor Wat was originally built as a temple for this religion.

_____ According to this religion's beliefs, a person's conduct determines the kind of life he or she is reborn into.

_____ This religion underwent a spiritual reform movement known as the Bhakti movement, which emphasized a personal devotion to a deity.

_____ This religion arrived in India through trade and through invasions.

_____ This religion spread throughout Central and East Asia via merchants and missionaries along the Silk Roads.

_____ Many Indians were converted to this religion by Sufi missionaries.

_____ Sacred texts of this religion are found in epic poems.

_____ This religion flourished under the Gupta Empire.

UNIT 4 CHAPTER 10 SECTION 1
Korea's Early History

VOCABULARY PRACTICE

KEY VOCABULARY

- **celadon** (SEH-luh-dahn) *n.* a type of Chinese pottery with a unique blue-green color

- **hanbok** (HAHN-bahk) *n.* a traditional Korean jacket and skirt or pant combination

- **kimchi** (KIM-chee) *n.* a spicy pickled vegetable mix that serves as Korea's national dish

- **ondol** (ON-dahl) *n.* a Korean system of heating in which an outside fire heats thick stones set into a floor.

FOUR-COLUMN CHART Complete a Four-Column Chart using each Key Vocabulary word. In the last column, use the word in a sentence.

Word	Definition	Illustration	Sentence
celadon			

NATIONAL
GEOGRAPHIC
LEARNING

UNIT 4

CHAPTER 10 SECTION 1

Korea's Early History

VOCABULARY PRACTICE

KEY VOCABULARY

- **adapt** *v.* to change
- **rivalry** *n.* a competition

I READ, I KNOW, AND SO Complete the charts below for the Key Vocabulary words *adapt* and *rivalry*. Write down the sentence in which the word appears. Then write down what else you read about the word. Finally, draw a conclusion about the word based on what you have learned.

I Read		
I Know	**adapt**	**And So**

I Read		
I Know	**rivalry**	**And So**

Chapter 10 SECTION 1 **ACTIVITY B** WORLD HISTORY

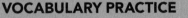

UNIT **4**

CHAPTER 10 SECTION 2
South and Southeast Asia

NATIONAL GEOGRAPHIC LEARNING

VOCABULARY PRACTICE

KEY VOCABULARY

- **bas-relief** (BAH ree-LEEF) *n.* a realistic sculpture with figures raised against a flat background

- **bodhisattva** (boh-dih-SUHT-vuh) *n.* an enlightened being who is worshipped as a god in Buddhism

- **golden age** *n.* a period of great cultural achievement

- **karma** (KAHR-mah) *n.* in Hinduism, a state of being influenced by a person's actions and conduct

- **reincarnation** (ree-ihn-kahr-NAY-shuhn) *n.* in Hinduism, the rebirth of a person's soul in another body after death

THREE-COLUMN CHART Complete the chart for each of the five Key Vocabulary words. Write each word's definition, and then provide a definition in your own words.

Word	Definition	In My Own Words
bas-relief		

UNIT 4 CHAPTER 10 SECTION 2
South and Southeast Asia

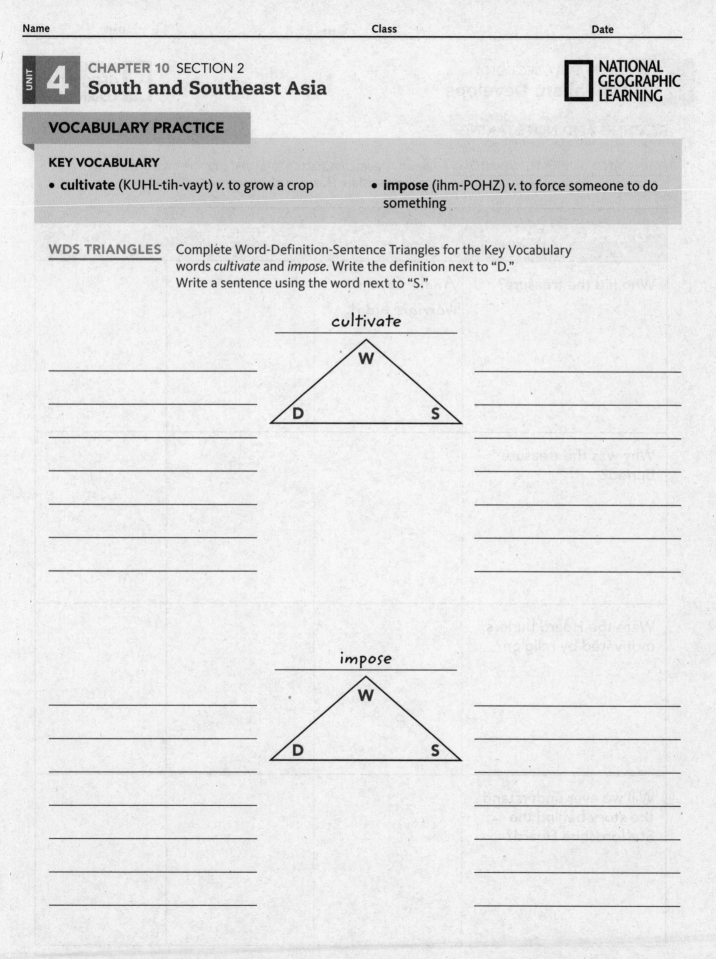

NATIONAL GEOGRAPHIC LEARNING

VOCABULARY PRACTICE

KEY VOCABULARY

- **cultivate** (KUHL-tih-vayt) *v.* to grow a crop

- **impose** (ihm-POHZ) *v.* to force someone to do something

WDS TRIANGLES Complete Word-Definition-Sentence Triangles for the Key Vocabulary words *cultivate* and *impose*. Write the definition next to "D." Write a sentence using the word next to "S."

cultivate

W

D   S

impose

W

D   S

READING AND NOTE-TAKING

FORM AND SUPPORT OPINIONS   Use an Argument Chart to form and support opinions about the Staffordshire Hoard, such as who buried it and why.

Questions to Answer	Viewpoint	Support	Opposing Viewpoint
Who hid the treasure?	Anglo-Saxon warriors hid it.		
Why was the treasure buried?			
Were the Hoard buriers motivated by religion?			
Will we ever understand the story behind the Staffordshire Hoard?			

CHAPTER 11 SECTION 1
Feudalism Develops

NATIONAL GEOGRAPHIC LEARNING

READING AND NOTE-TAKING

CATEGORIZE INFORMATION   Use Concept Clusters to organize information about Charlemagne and feudalism. Add more spokes to the outside circles to record additional information.

War

Administration

Social Hierarchy

Daily Life

Charlemagne

Feudalism

Religion

Manor System

UNIT **5** CHAPTER 11 SECTION 2
Political and Social Change

NATIONAL GEOGRAPHIC LEARNING

READING AND NOTE-TAKING

ANALYZE CAUSE AND EFFECT Complete a Cause-and-Effect Map to track the different developments that led to the decline of feudalism.

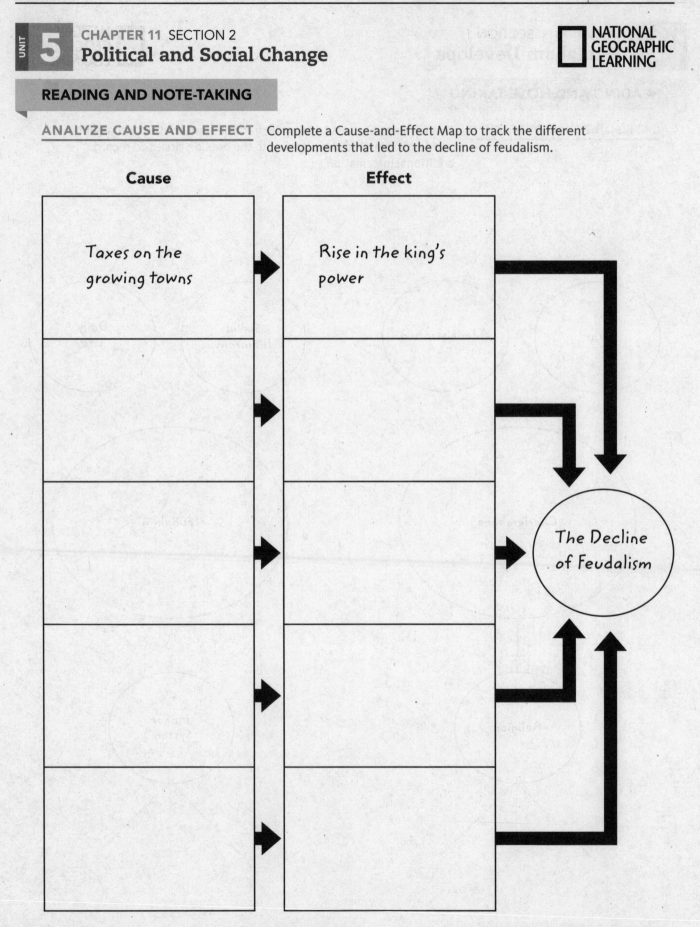

Cause

Effect

Taxes on the growing towns

Rise in the king's power

The Decline of Feudalism

CHAPTER 11 SECTION 2
Political and Social Change

NATIONAL
GEOGRAPHIC
LEARNING

READING AND NOTE-TAKING

CREATE A CHART Complete a chart to organize information about the various conflicts that arose in the Middle Ages, as discussed in Section 2.

Conflict	Key Dates	Details
King vs. Church	1075	

UNIT 5 CHAPTER 11 SECTION 1
Feudalism Develops

NATIONAL GEOGRAPHIC LEARNING

VOCABULARY PRACTICE

KEY VOCABULARY

- **chivalry** (SHIH-vuhl-ree) *n.* a code of conduct for knights
- **convert** *v.* to change one's religion

- **medieval** (muh-DEE-vuhl) *adj.* a period in history that spanned from the A.D. 500s to the 1500s; from the Latin *medium* (middle) and *aevum* (age)

WORD SQUARE Complete a Word Square for each Key Vocabulary word.

Definition	Characteristics
	chivalry
Examples	Non-Examples

Definition	Characteristics
Examples	Non-Examples

Definition	Characteristics
Examples	Non-Examples

UNIT 5 CHAPTER 11 SECTION 1
Feudalism Develops

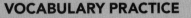

VOCABULARY PRACTICE

KEY VOCABULARY

- **feudalism** (FEW-duhl-ih-zuhm) *n.* a political and social system in which a vassal receives protection from a lord in exchange for obedience and service

- **knight** *n.* a warrior in medieval Europe

- **lord** *n.* a nobleman who received land from a king in medieval feudal society

- **manor** *n.* a self-contained world located on land belonging to a lord

- **serf** *n.* a person who lived and worked on the private land of a noble or medieval lord

- **vassal** (VASS-uhl) *n.* a person, usually a lesser nobleman, who received land and protection from a feudal lord in exchange for obedience and service

MANOR MAP Create a map of a medieval manor. Include the manor house and the places where you would find knights, lords, serfs, and vassals. Then add a caption to your illustration that explains what feudalism is. Be sure to include all the Key Vocabulary words in the caption to describe your map.

_____

_____

_____

_____

_____

Political and Social Change

NATIONAL GEOGRAPHIC LEARNING

VOCABULARY PRACTICE

KEY VOCABULARY

- **bubonic plague** (byoo-BAHN-ihk PLAYG) *n.* a disease that killed more than a third of Europe's population during the Middle Ages

- **burgher** (BUHR-guhr) *n.* a wealthy, town-dwelling merchant during the Middle Ages

- **guild** *n.* a group of craftspeople that helped protect and improve the working conditions of its members

- **longbow** *n.* a weapon that allowed archers to fire arrows

DEFINITION TREE For each Key Vocabulary word in the Tree Diagrams below, write the definition on the top branch and then use each word in a sentence.

bubonic plague

Definition
a disease that killed more than a third of Europe's population during the Middle Ages

Sentence
_____
_____
_____

burgher

Definition
_____
_____
_____

Sentence
_____
_____
_____

guild

Definition
_____
_____

Sentence
_____
_____
_____

longbow

Definition
_____
_____

Sentence
_____
_____
_____

UNIT 5

CHAPTER 11 SECTION 2
Political and Social Change

NATIONAL GEOGRAPHIC LEARNING

VOCABULARY PRACTICE

KEY VOCABULARY

- **cathedral** (kuh-THEE-druhl) *n.* a towering church built during the Middle Ages; often the place from which a bishop ruled
- **clergy** (KLUHR-gee) *n.* the religious leaders who oversee the ceremonies and deliver teachings of the Christian Church

- **common law** *n.* a system of law established in England to make sure people received equal treatment
- **monastery** (MAH-nuh-stair-ee) *n.* a Christian religious community
- **parliament** (PAHR-luh-ment) *n.* a group of representatives who shared power with the English monarch

WORDS IN CONTEXT Follow the directions for using the Key Vocabulary words in context.

1. Describe what a *cathedral* is.

_____

_____

2. Write the definition of *clergy* using your own words.

_____

_____

_____

3. Explain what a *monastery* is and what purpose it served in medieval Europe.

_____

_____

_____

4. Write the sentence in which the word *common law* appears in the lesson.

_____

_____

_____

5. Write the definition of *parliament* and explain what it does.

_____

_____

_____

Chapter 11 SECTION 2 **ACTIVITY B** WORLD HISTORY

BIOGRAPHY

JOAN OF ARC

Joan of Arc was a national heroine in France during the Hundred Years' War. Her legend lived well beyond her young life. Five hundred years after her death, the Catholic Church sainted her.

- **Job:** Soldier, Martyr, Saint
- **Qualities:** Persistence, Courage
- **Posthumous Honor:** Sainthood in 1920

Joan of Arc was born in the French village of Domrémy in 1412, during the Hundred Years' War between the French and the English. The English had occupied northern France. The heir to the French throne, Charles VII, called the Dauphin, had not yet been crowned king. Reims, the city in which the coronation traditionally took place, was in the hands of the English.

When Joan was 13 years old, she claimed that she experienced visions and heard the voices of Christian saints. At first, she told no one of her visions. But then she told her parents that the saints had commanded her to go see the Dauphin. She believed she was supposed to tell him to march to Reims so that he could finally be crowned king of France. Her parents refused to let her go, but Joan continued to have visions and her belief grew stronger. So she dressed in boy's clothing and, together with her brothers and others, she traveled on horseback to the Dauphin's quarters. The Dauphin was initially suspicious of her. Eventually, though, he provided Joan with armor, several attendants, and more horses.

She did not lead the army, but Joan of Arc's courageous presence inspired the French soldiers. The army moved into the city of Orléans and successfully took it back from the English. Next to fall to the French was Reims, where

A 19th-century painting of
Joan of Arc (1412–1431)

Joan of Arc, 1865 (oil on canvas), Millais, Sir John Everett (1829–96)/Private Collection/Photo © Peter Nahum at The Leicester Galleries, London/Bridgeman Images

the Dauphin was finally crowned as King Charles VII. The war continued, and in 1430 the English army captured Joan of Arc.

The English charged Joan of Arc with heresy and witchcraft. Her imprisonment included long periods of questioning and torture. The court sentenced her to death, and in 1431, at just 19 years of age, she was burned at the stake. In 1920, five hundred years after she was executed, the Roman Catholic Church declared Joan of Arc a saint.

REVIEW & ASSESS

1. **Summarize** What did Joan of Arc claim the saints told her to do?

_____

_____

2. **Make Inferences** Why did the English charge Joan of Arc with heresy and witchcraft?

_____

_____

Charters of Freedom

NATIONAL
GEOGRAPHIC
LEARNING

DOCUMENT-BASED QUESTION

Use the questions here to help you analyze the sources and write your paragraph.

DOCUMENT ONE: from the Magna Carta

1A Whose rights are protected in this passage from the Magna Carta?

_____

_____

1B Constructed Response What individual rights are protected in this article from the Magna Carta?

_____

_____

DOCUMENT TWO: from the English Bill of Rights

2A What freedom is protected and for whom in statement #8?

_____

_____

2B Constructed Response Why do you think Parliament insisted on the free election and free speech of its members?

_____

_____

DOCUMENT THREE: from the U.S. Bill of Rights

3A What personal freedoms are protected in statement #6?

_____

_____

3B Constructed Response Why do you think the American Founders insisted on having these freedoms clearly stated in the Bill of Rights?

_____

_____

SYNTHESIZE & WRITE

How do the Magna Carta, English Bill of Rights, and U.S. Bill of Rights promote democratic ideas?

Topic Sentence: _____

_____

Your Paragraph: _____

_____

_____

UNIT 5
CHAPTER 12 SECTION 1
The Italian Renaissance

READING AND NOTE-TAKING

IDENTIFY EFFECTS OF HUMANISM 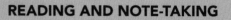 Complete a three-column chart to help organize your notes about the impact of humanism on different areas of European arts, science, and learning.

AREA	DEVELOPMENT	IMPACT
Art	*Artists moved from religious subjects to secular subjects.* ➡	
Literature	➡	
Architecture	➡	
Science	➡	
Learning	➡	

UNIT **5** CHAPTER 12 SECTION 1
The Italian Renaissance

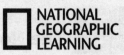
NATIONAL GEOGRAPHIC LEARNING

READING AND NOTE-TAKING

MAKE CONNECTIONS   Use the graphic organizer below to show the relationship between patrons' roles in politics and the Church and their ability to support the arts.

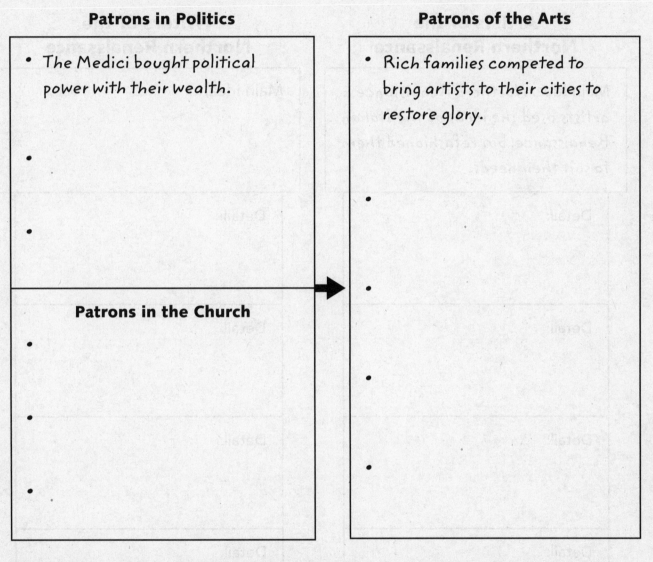

Patrons in Politics

- The Medici bought political power with their wealth.
-
-

Patrons in the Church

-
-
-

Patrons of the Arts

- Rich families competed to bring artists to their cities to restore glory.
-
-
-
-

Make Connections   What is the link between patrons' involvment in politics and the Church and the success of artists during the Renaissance?

_____

_____

_____

_____

Chapter 12 SECTION 1 **ACTIVITY B**   WORLD HISTORY

UNIT 5 — CHAPTER 12 SECTION 2
The Northern Renaissance

READING AND NOTE-TAKING

IDENTIFY MAIN IDEA AND DETAILS Complete Main Idea and Details Charts to organize information about artists and writers of the Northern Renaissance.

Artists of the Northern Renaissance

Main Idea: Northern Renaissance artists used the ideas of the Italian Renaissance, but refashioned them to suit their needs.

Detail:

Detail:

Detail:

Detail:

Detail:

Writers of the Northern Renaissance

Main Idea:

Detail:

Detail:

Detail:

Detail:

Detail:

UNIT 5 — CHAPTER 12 SECTION 2
The Northern Renaissance

NATIONAL GEOGRAPHIC LEARNING

READING AND NOTE-TAKING

ANALYZE CAUSE AND EFFECT   Complete a Cause-And-Effect Map to analyze the causes and effects associated with advances in printing technology during the Renaissance.

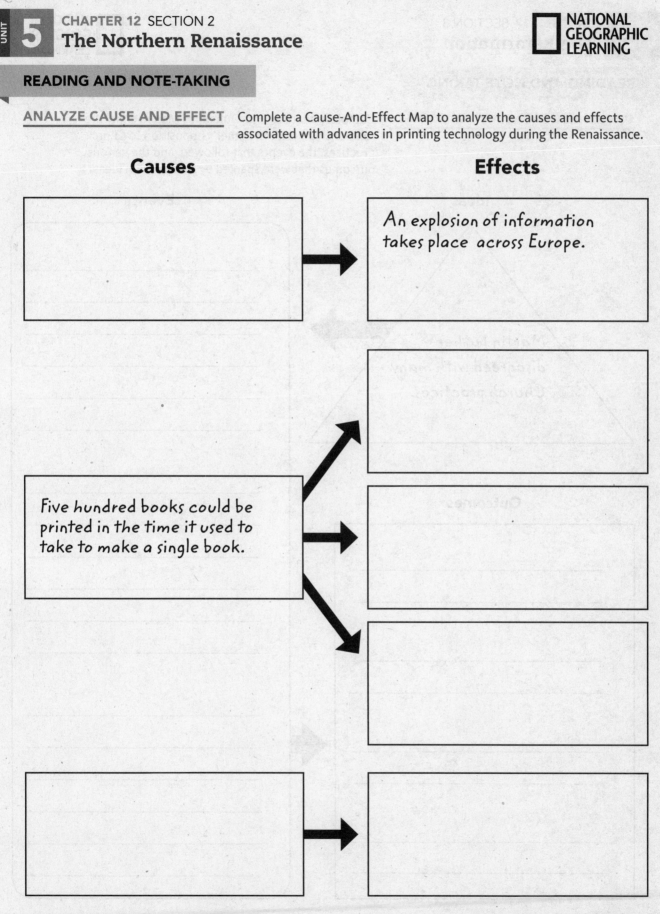

Causes   **Effects**

An explosion of information takes place across Europe.

Five hundred books could be printed in the time it used to take to make a single book.

Chapter 12 SECTION 2 **ACTIVITY B**   WORLD HISTORY

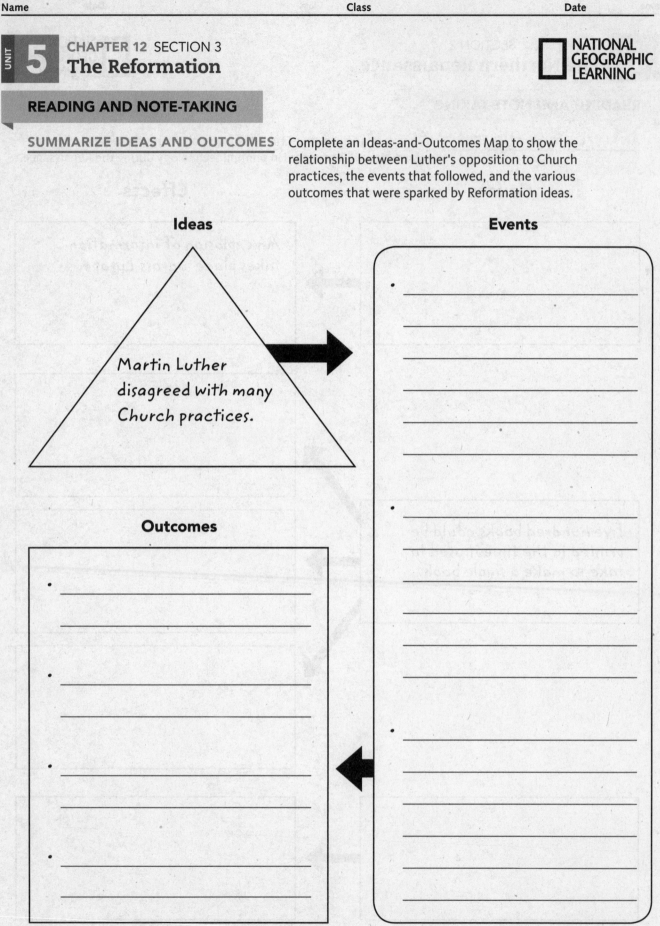

UNIT
5 CHAPTER 12 SECTION 3
The Reformation

**NATIONAL
GEOGRAPHIC
LEARNING**

READING AND NOTE-TAKING

SUMMARIZE IDEAS AND OUTCOMES Complete an Ideas-and-Outcomes Map to show the relationship between Luther's opposition to Church practices, the events that followed, and the various outcomes that were sparked by Reformation ideas.

Ideas

Martin Luther disagreed with many Church practices.

Events

Outcomes

CHAPTER 12 SECTION 3
The Reformation

READING AND NOTE-TAKING

OUTLINE AND TAKE NOTES   Complete an outline with notes on the Counter Reformation that took place in response to the Protestant Reformation.

I. <u>Catholic Church</u>

   A. <u>The Council of Trent met twice a year for 18 years to determine how the Church needed to change.</u>

   B. _____

     _____

   C. _____

     _____

   D. _____

     _____

II. <u>The Jesuits</u>

   A. _____

     _____

   B. _____

     _____

   C. _____

     _____

   D. _____

     _____

UNIT 5

CHAPTER 12 SECTION 1
The Italian Renaissance

NATIONAL GEOGRAPHIC LEARNING

VOCABULARY PRACTICE

KEY VOCABULARY

- **classical** *adj.* relating to ancient Greek and Roman culture

- **humanism** *n.* a movement that focused on the importance of the individual

- **patron** (PAY-truhn) *n.* a wealthy person who financially supports and encourages an artist

- **Renaissance man** (REHN-uh-sahns) *n.* a person who has a vide variety of skills and knowledge

THREE-COLUMN CHART Complete the chart for each of the four Key Vocabulary words. Write the word's definition, and then provide a definition in your own words.

Word	Definition	In My Own Words
classical		

UNIT 5 — CHAPTER 12 SECTION 1
The Italian Renaissance

NATIONAL GEOGRAPHIC LEARNING

VOCABULARY PRACTICE

KEY VOCABULARY

- **perspective** (puhr-SPEK-tihv) *n.* an artistic technique that produces an impression of depth and distance

- **secular** (SEHK-yoo-luhr) *adj.* nonreligious

- **vernacular** (vuhr-NAH-kyoo-lahr) *n.* a person's native language

RELATED IDEA WEB   Write one of the Key Vocabulary words inside each circle, along with its definition in your own words. Then draw lines or arrows connecting the circles to show how the words are related, based on what you read in Lesson 1.2. Write your explanation of the connection next to the line or arrow.

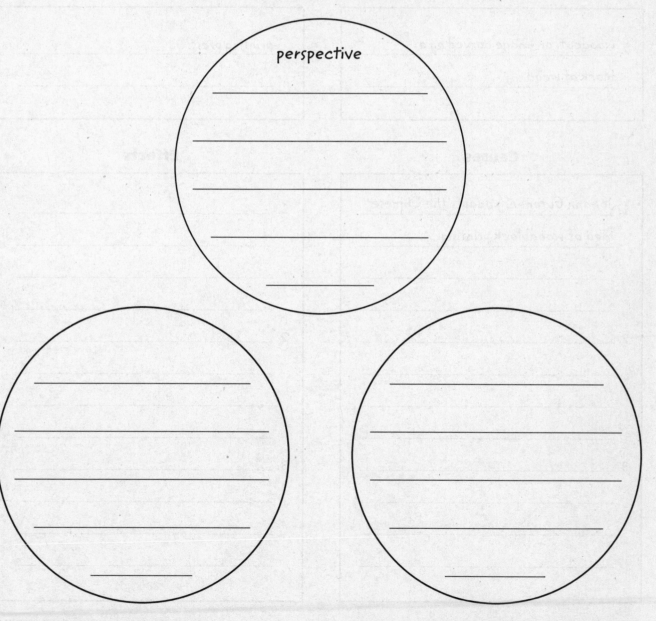

perspective

UNIT 5

CHAPTER 12 SECTION 2
The Northern Renaissance

VOCABULARY PRACTICE

KEY VOCABULARY

- **printing press** *n.* an invention that used movable metal type to print pages
- **woodcut** *n.* an image carved on a block of wood

CAUSE-AND-EFFECT CHART   Define the Key Vocabulary words *woodcut* and *printing press*. Then complete a Cause-and-Effect Chart with at least two causes and two effects that show how the words are related.

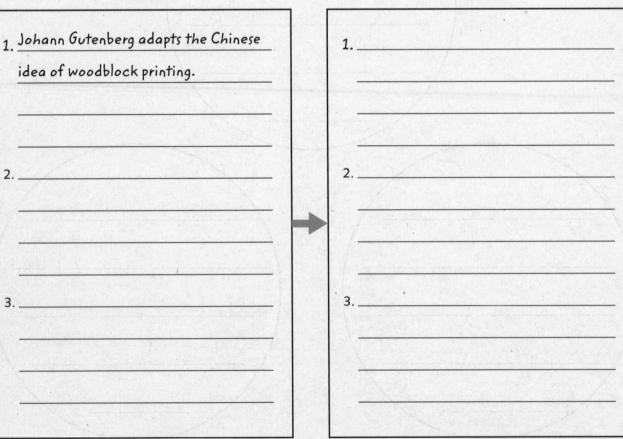

Definition

woodcut: an image carved on a
block of wood

Definition

printing press:

Causes

1. Johann Gutenberg adapts the Chinese idea of woodblock printing.

2.

3.

Effects

1.

2.

3.

UNIT 5 CHAPTER 12 SECTION 2
The Northern Renaissance

NATIONAL GEOGRAPHIC LEARNING

VOCABULARY PRACTICE

KEY VOCABULARY

• **cartography** (KAHR-tah-grah-fee) *n.* the study of maps and mapmaking

CARTOGRAPHY PROJECT Create a simple map of a your school, neighborhood, house, shopping mall, or other real world place. While drawing your map, try to keep the sizes of objects proportionate. For example, if you are drawing your school, your classroom should fit the relative size within the building. Label features on your map. Below your map, use the Key Vocabulary word in a caption that describes how you made your map.

_____

_____

_____

Summarize Describe the process you used to create your map.

_____

_____

_____

_____

_____

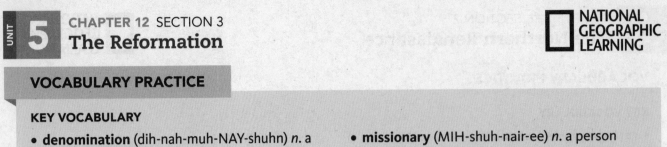

UNIT 5

CHAPTER 12 SECTION 3
The Reformation

NATIONAL GEOGRAPHIC LEARNING

VOCABULARY PRACTICE

KEY VOCABULARY

- **denomination** (dih-nah-muh-NAY-shuhn) *n.* a branch of one type of religion

- **heresy** (HAIR-uh-see) *n.* beliefs contrary to Church teachings; opposition to Church policy

- **indulgence** (in-DUHL-juhns) *n.* the release from punishment for sins, sold by papal officials

- **missionary** (MIH-shuh-nair-ee) *n.* a person who goes to another country to do religious work; a person who tries to spread Christianity to others

- **nation-state** *n.* a country with an independent government and a population united by a shared culture, language, and national pride; a political unit in which people have a common culture and identity

DEFINITION AND DETAILS Complete a Definition-and-Details Chart for the Key Vocabulary words. For each word, write the definition and two details related to the word, based on what you read in Section 3.

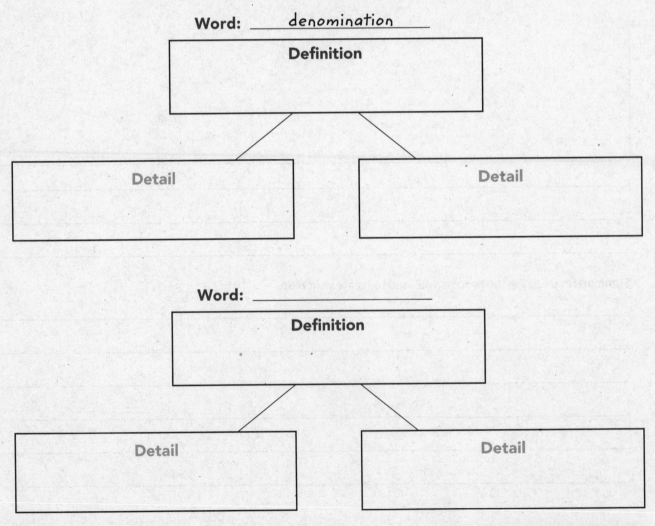

Word: _____denomination_____

Definition

Detail	Detail

Word: _____

Definition

Detail	Detail

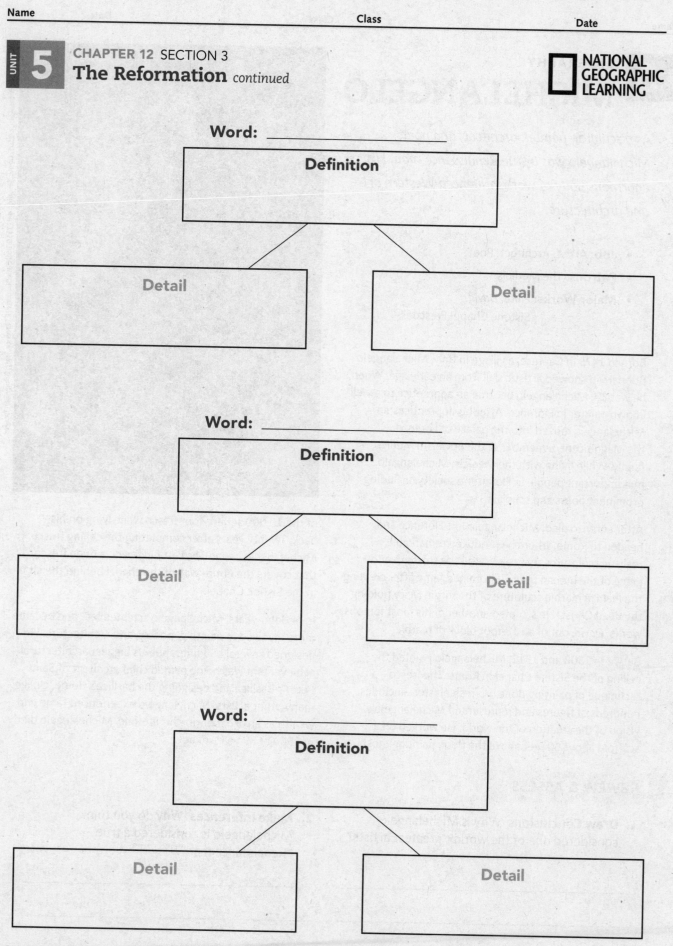

Word: _____

Definition

Detail

Detail

Word: _____

Definition

Detail

Detail

Word: _____

Definition

Detail

Detail

BIOGRAPHY
MICHELANGELO

As a sculptor, painter, architect, and poet, Michelangelo was a true Renaissance man. His enormous body of work influenced Western art and architecture.

- **Job:** Artist, Architect, Poet
- **Patrons:** The Medicis
- **Major Works:** *Pietá*, *David*, Sistene Chapel Frescoes

Born in 1475 in Caprese, a village in Italy, Michelangelo Buonarroti showed artistic skill from an early age. When he was 13, Michelangelo became an apprentice to a well known painter in Florence. After his apprenticeship, Michelangelo moved into the palace of Lorenzo the Magnificent, a member of the powerful Medici family. While living with the Medicis, Michelangelo met important people in Florentine society, including prominent poets and scholars.

After Lorenzo died, Michelangelo left Florence and headed to Rome, where he produced remarkable, realistic sculptures that celebrated the strength and grace of the human figure. He gained fame after creating the *Pietá*, a marble sculpture of the Virgin Mary holding the dead Christ. He sculpted another of his most famous works, *David*, out of an 18-foot block of marble.

Between 1508 and 1512, Michelangelo painted the ceiling of the Sistine Chapel in Rome. The fresco—a technique of painting done on fresh plaster—includes hundreds of figures and represented Michelangelo's vision of the creation of the world. He worked on a scaffold about 60 feet above the floor, painting most

Portrait of Michelangelo, c.1535, Conte, Jacopino del (1510-98)/Casa Buonarroti, Florence, Italy/Bridgeman Images

Portrait of Michelangelo (1475–1564) by Jacopino del Conte, c. 1535

of the 10,000 square-foot fresco while lying on his back. Twenty years after completing the ceiling fresco, Michelangelo began *The Last Judgment*, a huge fresco that covers the entire wall of the chapel behind the altar in the Sistine Chapel.

In his later years, Michelangelo sculpted less and became more involved in painting, poetry, and architecture. He designed several buildings, but his biggest architectural achievement was being named chief architect of Saint Peter's Basilica and designing the basilica's dome. Unlike many other artists, Michelangelo experienced fame and wealth as an artist during his lifetime. Michelangelo died in 1564 at 89 years of age.

REVIEW & ASSESS

1. **Draw Conclusions** Why is Michelangelo considered one of the world's greatest artists?

2. **Make Inferences** Why do you think Michelangelo is considered a true "Renaissance man"?

© National Geographic Learning, Cengage Learning

UNIT 5 BIOGRAPHY
MARTIN
LUTHER

Martin Luther was a monk who questioned some of the basic principles of the Roman Catholic Church. His ideas launched the Protestant Reformation and the beginnings of Protestantism.

- **Job:** Professor of Biblical Literature
- **Pet Peeve:** Indulgences, Church Corruption
- **Bravest Moment:** Posting the 95 Theses

Martin Luther was born in the German town of Eisleben in 1483. Though he initially studied law, he later chose a religious life as a monk. As a monk, Luther's life involved daily work and worship. He lived in unheated, small quarters with only a table and chair. Luther became and outstanding student of theology and a respected biblical scholar. He earned a doctorate in theology and became a professor of biblical literature at Wittenberg University in Germany. After his in-depth study of the Bible, Luther came to believe that the key to salvation was to believe that faith in God alone.

In 1517 a conflict developed between Martin Luther and the Catholic Church. Pope Leo X wanted to raise money to build Saint Peter's Basilica in Rome. To raise the funds, he offered to sell indulgences, which were, in effect, payments for the forgiveness of sins. Luther opposed this practice and he posted a list of protests known as the 95 Theses. The list included the idea that the Bible was the only source of religious truth and that only God could forgive. Not surprisingly, Luther's actions angered the pope, who excommunicated him in 1521. Luther

Monument for Martin Luther (1483–1546) in Wittenberg, Germany

was convicted as a heretic and outlawed. To escape the conviction, Luther hid in a castle at Wartburg. While there he began to translate the Bible from Latin into German. When it was safe to come out of hiding, Luther returned to his university job at Wittenberg.

In 1525, Luther married, again rejecting the teachings of the Roman Catholic Church. He and his wife had five children. Luther spent the rest of his life writing, teaching, and preaching. Martin Luther died in 1546.

REVIEW & ASSESS

1. **Analyze Cause and Effect** What prompted Martin Luther to post the 95 Theses?

_____

_____

2. **Make Inferences** Why is Martin Luther considered an influential person in history of the Christian church?

_____

_____

UNIT 5

CHAPTER 12 · LESSON 3.2
Conflict in the Church

NATIONAL GEOGRAPHIC LEARNING

DOCUMENT-BASED QUESTION

Use the questions here to help you analyze the sources and write your paragraph.

DOCUMENT ONE: from the 95 Theses

1A According to the passage, how does "man become better"?

_____

_____

1B Constructed Response Why might the Church have taken offense at these statements?

_____

DOCUMENT TWO: from the Papal Bull of Pope Leo X

2A In this passage, to whom does "we" refer?

_____

_____

2B Constructed Response According to the pope, how should Catholics deal with Luther's ideas?

_____

DOCUMENT THREE: Leaflet Against Johann Tetzel

3A In your own words, explain what Tetzel is selling.

_____

_____

3B Constructed Response Why do you think the people shown in the leaflet are happy to see Tetzel?

_____

SYNTHESIZE & WRITE

How did the Church and Luther's followers react to the 95 Theses?

Topic Sentence: _____

_____

Your Paragraph: _____

_____

_____

_____

_____

UNIT 5
CHAPTER 13 SECTION 1
The Scientific Revolution

READING AND NOTE-TAKING

ANALYZE CAUSE AND EFFECT As you read Section 1, complete a flow chart to show how knowledge advanced from a geocentric theory to a heliocentric theory of the universe.

Heliocentric Theory of the Universe

First:

Ancient Greek thinkers believed Earth was at the center of our universe.

↓

Next:

↓

Last:

UNIT 5

CHAPTER 13 SECTION 1
The Scientific Revolution

READING AND NOTE-TAKING

MAKE CONNECTIONS   After you read Section 1, complete a T-Chart to match scientists with scientific advances listed at the bottom of the page. Note that some of the scientific advances may apply to more than one scientist.

SCIENTISTS	ADVANCES
A. Newton	*law of universal gravitation*
B. Hooke	
C. Muslim scholars	
D. Copernicus	
E. Boyle	
F. Bacon	
G. Descartes	
H. Galileo	

scientific rationalism, all matter is made of up of particles, first to name and describe cells, influenced a European revolution in science, law of universal gravitation, brought together learning from other cultures, sun-centered universe, color wheel

Chapter 13 SECTION 1 **ACTIVITY B**   WORLD HISTORY

UNIT 5 CHAPTER 13 SECTION 2
The Age of Exploration

READING AND NOTE-TAKING

SEQUENCE EXPLORATION As you read about the age of exploration in Section 2, complete a chart with notes on the beginnings of European exploration.

Country	Year	Event
Portugal	1419	Explored Africa's western coast, established trading ports

UNIT **5** CHAPTER 13 SECTION 2
The Age of Exploration

NATIONAL GEOGRAPHIC LEARNING

READING AND NOTE-TAKING

CATEGORIZE INFORMATION After reading about the Columbian Exchange in Lesson 2.5, complete a Concept Cluster with information about the kinds of products that moved from the old world to the new. Add more spokes to your circles as needed.

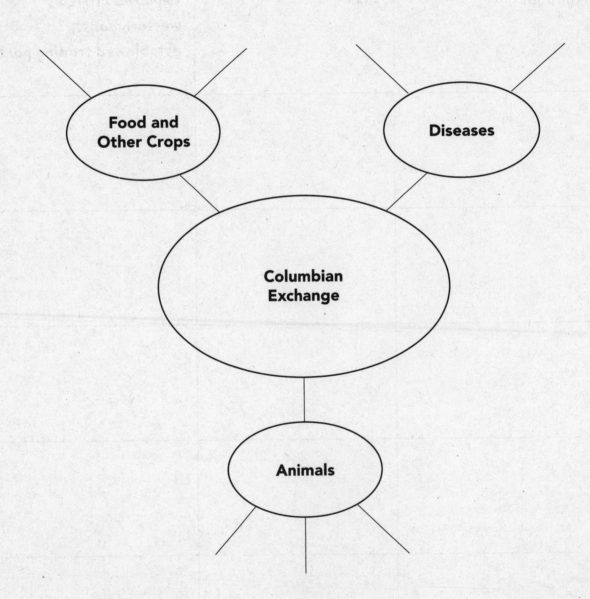

UNIT 5 | CHAPTER 13 SECTION 3
European Empires

READING AND NOTE-TAKING

SYNTHESIZE VISUAL AND TEXTUAL INFORMATION   As you read Lesson 3.1 take note of the Rivera mural featured in the lesson. Then answer the questions below.

1. What were the Spanish seeking in the new world?

_____

_____

2. What is the title of the mural?

_____

_____

3. According to the text, why did some native people march with Cortés against the Aztec?

_____

_____

4. What are people doing in the background of the mural?

_____

_____

5. What are the people doing in the foreground of the mural?

_____

_____

6. When was the mural painted?

_____

_____

7. How long did the Spanish rule Mexico?

_____

_____

8. When did they move into Biru from Mexico?

_____

_____

UNIT 5

CHAPTER 13 SECTION 3
European Empires

NATIONAL GEOGRAPHIC LEARNING

READING AND NOTE-TAKING

OUTLINE AND TAKE NOTES As you read Section 3.3 use the outline below to organize and keep track of the important information you read.

What is the title of the lesson? _____

What is the Main Idea? _____

_____

_____

What is the "Slave Labor" passage about? _____ _____ _____	What is the "Impact of the Slave Trade" passage about? _____ _____ _____
What does the illustration show? _____ _____ _____	What does the inset of the illustration show? _____ _____ _____

Synthesize The Atlantic slave trade had a great impact on the world. What do you think is the most important thing to remember from the lesson?

_____

_____

_____

_____

UNIT **5**

CHAPTER 13 SECTION 1
The Scientific Revolution

**NATIONAL
GEOGRAPHIC
LEARNING**

VOCABULARY PRACTICE

KEY VOCABULARY

- **elliptical** (ee-LIHP-tih-kuhl) *adj.* oval

- **geocentric theory** (JEE-oh-sehn-trihk THEER-ee) *n.* a theory that places Earth at the center of the universe

- **heliocentric theory** (HEE-lee-oh-sehn-trihk THEER-ee) *n.* a theory that places the sun at the center of the universe

PICTURE DICTIONARY   Create a dictionary page of Scientific Revolution terms. Include the pronunciation, the definition, and an illustration for each of the three Key Vocabulary words.

elliptical (ee-LIHP-tih-kuhl)

_____

_____

_____

_____

_____

_____

_____

_____

_____

_____

_____

UNIT 5

CHAPTER 13 SECTION 1
The Scientific Revolution

NATIONAL
GEOGRAPHIC
LEARNING

VOCABULARY PRACTICE

KEY VOCABULARY

- **hypothesis** (hy-PAHTH-uh-sihs) *n.* an explanation that can be tested

- **scientific method** *n.* a logical procedure for developing and testing ideas

- **scientific rationalism** *n.* a school of thought in which observation, experimentation, and mathematical reasoning replace ancient wisdom and church teachings as the source of scientific truth

- **theory** (THEER-ee) *n.* a proposed explanation for a set of facts

WORDS IN CONTEXT   Follow the directions for using the Key Vocabulary words in context.

1. Write the sentence in which the word *hypothesis* appears in the section.

_____

_____

_____

_____

2. Describe the five steps of the *scientific method*.

_____

_____

_____

_____

3. Use the word *theory* in a sentence of your own.

_____

_____

_____

_____

4. Explain what *scientific rationalism* is and how it was used.

_____

_____

_____

_____

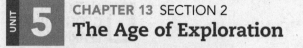

UNIT 5

CHAPTER 13 SECTION 2
The Age of Exploration

NATIONAL GEOGRAPHIC LEARNING

VOCABULARY PRACTICE

KEY VOCABULARY

- **caravel** (KAIR-uh-vehl) *n.* a small, fast ship used by early European explorers
- **colony** (KAH-luh-nee) *n.* a group of people who settle in a new land but keep ties to their native country
- **exploit** (EHKS-ployt) *v.* to mistreat
- **rivalry** (RY-vuhl-ree) *n.* a competition

WDS CHART   Complete a Word-Definition-Sentence (WDS) Chart for each Key Vocabulary word.

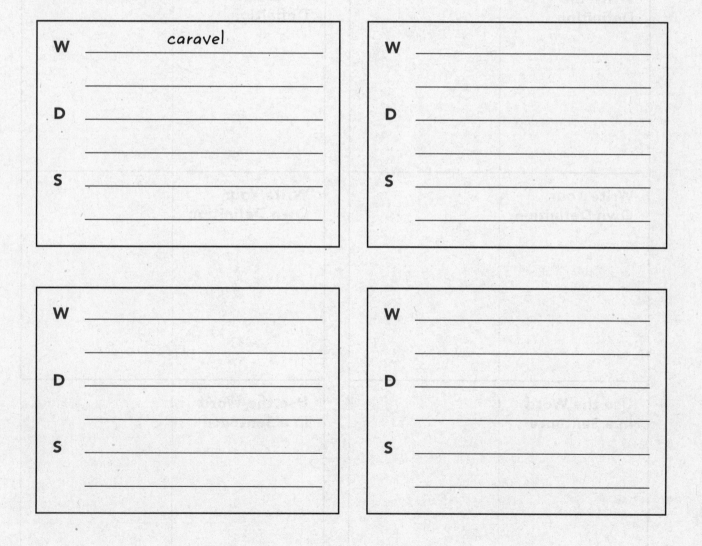

W _____ caravel _____
_____
D _____
_____
S _____
_____

W _____
_____
D _____
_____
S _____
_____

W _____
_____
D _____
_____
S _____
_____

W _____
_____
D _____
_____
S _____
_____

UNIT 5
CHAPTER 13 SECTION 2
The Age of Exploration

VOCABULARY PRACTICE

KEY VOCABULARY

- **quinine** (KWY-nine) *n.* a substance from the bark of a tree that is an effective remedy for malaria

- **smallpox** *n.* a deadly virus that causes a high fever and small blisters on the skin

DEFINITION CHART   Complete a Definition Chart for the Key Vocabulary words.

Word	quinine
Write the Definition	
Write Your Own Definition	
Use the Word in a Sentence	

Word	smallpox
Write the Definition	
Write Your Own Definition	
Use the Word in a Sentence	

CHAPTER 13 SECTION 3
European Empires

**NATIONAL
GEOGRAPHIC
LEARNING**

VOCABULARY PRACTICE

KEY VOCABULARY

- **conquistador** (kahn-KEES-tuh-dawr) *n.* a Spanish conqueror who was looking for gold and other riches in the Americas

VOCABULARY PYRAMID Complete a Vocabulary Pyramid for the Key Vocabulary word *conquistador*.

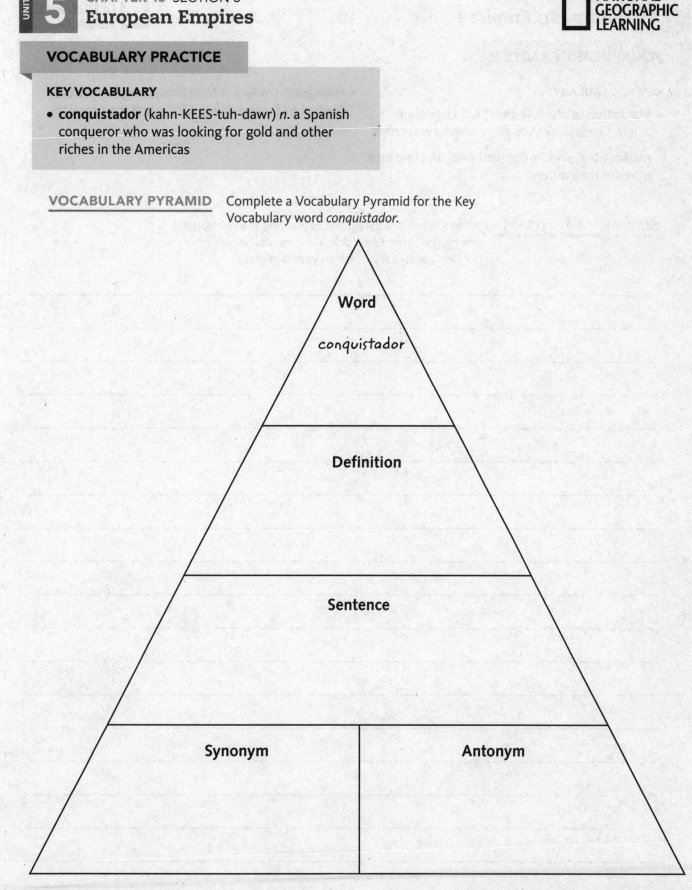

Word

conquistador

Definition

Sentence

Synonym

Antonym

UNIT 5 CHAPTER 13 SECTION 3
European Empires

VOCABULARY PRACTICE

KEY VOCABULARY

- **plantation** (plahn-TAY-shun) *n.* a large farm where slaves worked to grow and harvest crops

- **racism** (RAY-sih-zihm) *n.* the belief that one race is better than others

- **triangular trade** *n.* a transatlantic trade network formed by Europe, West Africa, and the Americas

SUMMARY PARAGRAPH   Write a summary paragraph explaining the relationship among the three Key Vocabulary words. Use all of the Key Vocabulary words in your summary.

_____

_____

_____

_____

_____

_____

_____

_____

_____

_____

_____

_____

_____

_____

_____

_____

_____

UNIT 5

BIOGRAPHY
GALILEO
GALILEI

Galileo Galilei was the first astronomer to use a telescope to study the universe. His revolutionary ideas led to condemnation by the Roman Catholic Church. His work laid the foundation for modern physics and astronomy.

- **Job:** Scientist, Mathematician, Astronomer
- **Rejected:** Aristotelian Theory
- **Supported:** Copernican Theory

A 19th-century painting of Galileo Galilei (1564–1642)

Galileo was born in Pisa, Italy, in 1564. He first studied medicine, but then his interest turned to science and mathematics. In 1589, he became the lecturer on mathematics at the University of Pisa. At that time, scientists—and the Roman Catholic Church—supported the view of the world as taught by Aristotle many centuries before.

Galileo began making enemies with the Church when he argued that Aristotelian science was flawed. For example, through his experiments, Galileo showed that all objects fall at the same rate. His conclusion opposed Aristotle's theory that heavy objects fall at faster rates than lighter objects. Galileo's ideas so angered others that he was forced to leave Pisa in 1591.

Galileo soon learned that a Dutch eyeglass maker had invented a simple telescope. So in 1609, Galileo built his own telescope and began to study the universe. He recorded his observations in a pamphlet titled *The Starry Messenger*. Galileo supported the Copernican theory

that the sun, not Earth, was the center of the universe. In 1632 he published *Dialogue Concerning the Two Chief World Systems*. Because of the ideas he proposed, Church officials called him to Rome where they questioned him for nearly a year. He did not take back his claims. Finally, threatened with torture, Galileo announced his rejection of the Copernican theory. In private, however, Galileo continued to support it. The Church convicted him of heresy, and he spent the remaining years of his life under house arrest until his death in 1642.

In 1758 the Church lifted the ban on most works that supported the Copernican theory, and in 1835 it dropped its opposition completely. In 1992, Pope John Paul II expressed regret about the Church's treatment of Galileo.

REVIEW & ASSESS

1. **Summarize** Which worldview did Galileo reject and which did he support?

_____

_____

2. **Analyze Cause and Effect** How did the Church respond to Galileo's *Dialogue Concerning the Two Chief World Systems?*

_____

_____

UNIT 5

CHAPTER 13 LESSON 2.4
A New World

DOCUMENT-BASED QUESTION

Use the questions here to help you analyze the sources and write your paragraph.

DOCUMENT ONE: from *The Journal of Christopher Columbus*

1A What does Columbus tell the Spanish monarchs he plans to do?

_____

_____

_____

1B Constructed Response What land was Columbus trying to reach, and what was unusual about his route?

_____

_____

_____

DOCUMENT TWO: Map from 1513

2A What parts of this map, if any, are recognizable to you?

_____

_____

_____

_____

2B Constructed Response What does this map demonstrate about European knowledge of the Western Hemisphere in 1513??

_____

_____

_____

SYNTHESIZE & WRITE

How did European voyages lead to unexpected results?

Topic Sentence: _____

_____

Your Paragraph: _____

_____

_____

_____

_____

UNIT 5 **CHAPTER 14 SECTION 1**
The Age of Reason

READING AND NOTE-TAKING

<u>CREATE A CHART</u> Complete a three-column chart to organize information about Enlightenment ideas, the philosophes behind them, and how these ideas changed people's lives.

Enlightenment Idea	Associated Philosophes	Proposed Societal Changes
Human reason should guide a person's actions, not tradition or religion.	Voltaire	

CHAPTER 14 SECTION 1
The Age of Reason

**NATIONAL
GEOGRAPHIC
LEARNING**

READING AND NOTE-TAKING

DRAW CONCLUSIONS Complete a chart to track the ways in which European rulers applied
and rejected Enlightment ideas. Then answer the question.

Applied Enlightenment Ideas	Rejected Enlightenment Ideas
• Frederick the Great introduced religious tolerance and legal reforms in Prussia.	• Frederick the Great
• Joseph II	
	• Catherine the Great
• Catherine the Great	

Draw Conclusions Did the changes that the European rulers chose to make
during the Enlightenment satisfy the philosophes?

_____

_____

_____

_____

_____

Chapter 14 SECTION 1 **ACTIVITY B** WORLD HISTORY

CHAPTER 14 SECTION 2
Two Revolutions

NATIONAL
GEOGRAPHIC
LEARNING

READING AND NOTE-TAKING

<u>ANALYZE REVOLUTIONS</u>   As you read about the American and French revolutions, complete a flow chart to help you analyze the information.

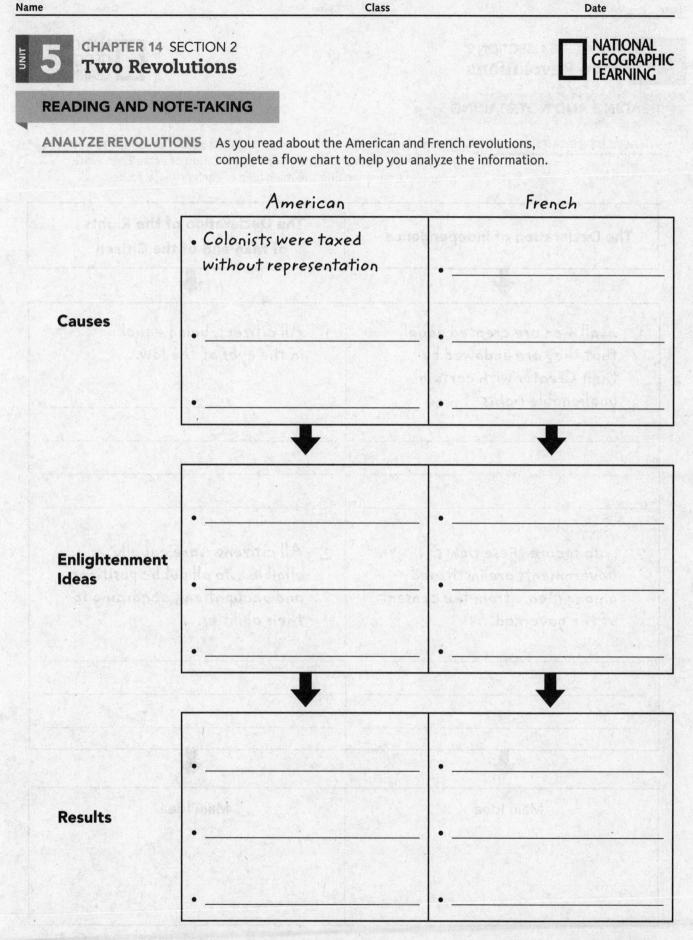

American

French

Causes

- Colonists were taxed without representation
- _____
- _____

- _____
- _____

Enlightenment Ideas

- _____
- _____
- _____

- _____
- _____
- _____

Results

- _____
- _____
- _____

- _____
- _____
- _____

UNIT 5

CHAPTER 14 SECTION 2
Two Revolutions

NATIONAL
GEOGRAPHIC
LEARNING

READING AND NOTE-TAKING

ANALYZE PRIMARY SOURCES Complete a chart to analyze excerpts from two documents of revolution. Read the excerpts and write your interpretation of each. Then write a sentence summarizing the main idea of each primary source.

The Declaration of Independence	The Declaration of the Rights of Man and of the Citizen
1. ...all men are created equal, that they are endowed by their Creator with certain unalienable rights...	1. All citizens, being equal in the eyes of the law...
_____ _____ _____	_____ _____ _____
2. ...to secure these rights, Governments are instituted among Men...from the consent of the governed...	2. All citizens...are equally eligible...to all public positions and occupations, according to their abilities...
_____ _____ _____	_____ _____ _____
Main Idea	Main Idea

Chapter 14 SECTION 2 **ACTIVITY B** WORLD HISTORY

UNIT
5 CHAPTER 14 SECTION 1
The Age of Reason

VOCABULARY PRACTICE

KEY VOCABULARY

- **absolute monarch** *n.* a ruler who has unlimited authority

- **contract** *n.* an agreement between two or more people

- **divine right** *n.* a right to rule believed to be given by God to a king or queen

- **enlightened despot** (en-LYT-tenhd DEHS-puht) *n.* an absolute ruler who applied Enlightenment principles to his or her reign

- **free enterprise** *n.* an economic system in which people buying and selling products in markets determine what products are needed and what price should be paid for them

- **laissez-faire** (LEHS-ay FAYR) *n.* a policy that calls for less government involvement in economic affairs

FOUR-COLUMN CHART Complete the chart below for each Key Vocabulary word. In the last column, use the word in a sentence.

Word	Definition	In My Own Words
absolute monarch		

UNIT 5

CHAPTER 14 SECTION 1
The Age of Reason

VOCABULARY PRACTICE

KEY VOCABULARY

- **natural right** *n.* a right, such as life or liberty, that a person is born with

- **philosophe** (fee-loh-ZOHF) *n.* an Enlightenment thinker

- **reason** *n.* the power of the human mind to think and understand in a logical way

RELATED IDEA MAP Use a Related Idea Map to help you understand the relationships among three Key Vocabulary words. In the boxes, provide definitions of each Key Vocabulary word in your own words. Then draw lines between the boxes and add a sentence to explain how the words are related.

reason

UNIT 5

CHAPTER 14 SECTION 2
Two Revolutions

VOCABULARY PRACTICE

KEY VOCABULARY
- **bourgeoisie** (boor-jwah-ZEE) *n.* the middle class

WORD SQUARE   Complete a Word Square for the Key Vocabulary word.

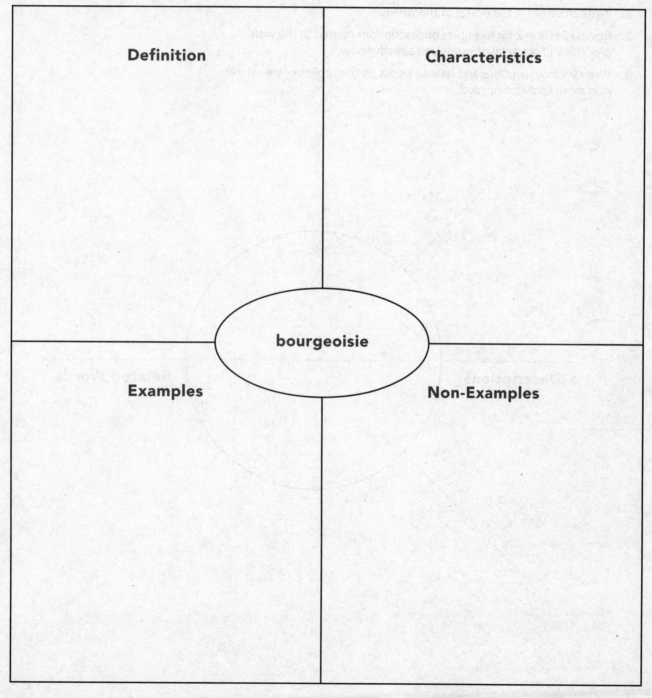

Definition

Characteristics

bourgeoisie

Examples

Non-Examples

UNIT 5

CHAPTER 14 SECTION 2
Two Revolutions

VOCABULARY PRACTICE

KEY VOCABULARY
- **bourgeoisie** (boor-jwah-ZEE) *n.* the middle class

WORD WHEEL   Follow the instructions below to analyze the Key Vocabulary word *bourgeoisie*.

1. Write the word in the center of the wheel.

2. Review Section 2 for examples of descriptions related to the word, and think of any related words you already know.

3. Write your descriptions and related words on the spokes of the wheel. Add more spokes if needed.

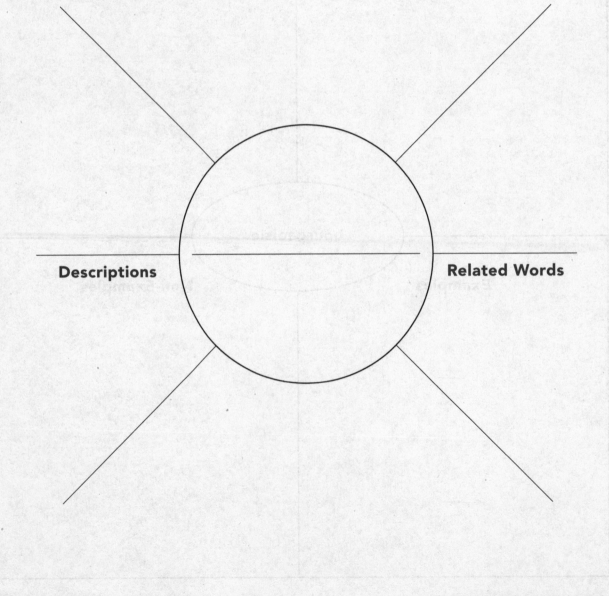

Descriptions   Related Words

©Alpha Historica/Alamy Stock Photo

UNIT 5 BIOGRAPHY
DR. MARTIN LUTHER KING, JR.

Civil rights activist Dr. Martin Luther King, Jr., was a Baptist minister who believed in peaceful, nonviolent protests to bring an end to racial discrimination.

- **Job:** Minister; Social Activist
- **Honors:** *Time* Magazine Man of the Year 1963; Nobel Peace Prize 1964
- **Influences:** Jesus Christ; Mohandas Gandhi

Portrait of Dr. Martin Luther King, Jr. (1929–1968)

Martin Luther King, Jr., was born on January 15, 1929, in Atlanta, Georgia, to a family deeply rooted in their Baptist faith. He grew up during a time when racial discrimination and inequalities were ever-present in our nation. After many years of questioning his religion, King enrolled in a seminary. Here he met Benjamin E. Mays, a staunch advocate for racial equality, who encouraged him to use Christianity to enact change. King later earned a doctoral degree at Boston University, where he met Coretta Scott, a musician and singer. The couple married in 1953 and had four children.

King became a pastor of the Dexter Avenue Baptist Church in Montgomery, Alabama, and, in 1955, completed his Ph.D. In December of that year, Rosa Parks was told to give up her seat on a bus for a white man. When she refused, Parks was arrested. Backed by other civil rights leaders, Martin Luther King, Jr., led a peaceful 381-day bus boycott in response. The group faced violence and discrimination, but the U.S. Supreme Court eventually ruled that public bus segregation was illegal.

After this victory, the Southern Christian Leadership Conference was formed. A key participant, King spoke out against racism and worked tirelessly to give African Americans a voice. In 1960, King and his family returned to Atlanta, Georgia. King continued to inspire people around the nation with his eloquent speeches and by using peaceful methods to achieve equality. On August 28, 1963, King gave his famous "I Have a Dream" speech during the March on Washington. One year later, he received the Nobel Peace Prize.

King worked throughout the 1960s to bring awareness to racial injustices. Some people said his approach was passive and ineffective, but hundreds of thousands believed in his message. On April 3, 1968, King gave his last speech. The next day, he was shot and killed by James Earl Ray in Memphis, Tennessee. In 1986, a federal holiday was named to honor the life and legacy of Dr. Martin Luther King, Jr.

REVIEW & ASSESS

1. **Make Connections** In what ways can you support the work of Dr. Martin Luther King, Jr., on his national holiday?

_____

_____

2. **Synthesize** How does the work of Dr. King reflect Enlightenment principles?

_____

_____

UNIT **5**

BIOGRAPHY

JOHN LOCKE

John Locke was a brilliant, Enlightenment theorist who wrote about politics, government, and psychology. His ideas helped inspire two revolutions that changed the political landscape.

- **Job:** Political Philosopher
- **Education:** Oxford University
- **Major Work:** *Two Treatises of Government,* "Essay Concerning Human Understanding"

John Locke was born in England in 1632. Both his parents were Puritans and raised Locke in that tradition. Locke was educated at Oxford University where he studied a wide variety of subjects, including logic and classical languages. His interest in science led him to study medicine, particularly medical research.

However, Locke is best known for his works on political philosophy, or the study of politics, law, and government. In his *Two Treatises of Government*, Locke argued that all people are born with certain rights, mainly the right to life, liberty, and property. Further, the purpose of government is to protect those rights and if it does not do so, then citizens have the right to overthrow the government. Locke argued that government should be a contract, or an agreement, between the ruler and the ruled and that rulers had power only through the consent of the people. Locke's political philosophy formed the basis of modern democracy. His *Two Treatises of Government* influenced revolutionaries in the American and French Revolutions, which took place 70 years after his death.

Portrait of John Locke (1632–1704)

In addition to his works on political philosophy, Locke was also interested in human psychology. In his "Essay Concerning Human Understanding," Locke asserted that human minds begin as blank slates, with no pre-set ideas. He argued that people form ideas through experience and that character formation is as important as academics in education.

Locke's political theories shaped the development of politics and government in 18th-century Europe and the American colonies. His ideas provided the foundation for the U.S. Constitution, and they continue to be an important part of modern politics and government. John Locke died in 1704.

REVIEW & ASSESS

1. **Summarize** According to Locke, what are the rights that all people are born with?

_____

_____

2. **Make Inferences** How did Locke's ideas help inspire the American and French Revolutions?

_____

_____

UNIT 5 BIOGRAPHY
CATHERINE
THE GREAT

Catherine the Great ruled Russia from 1762 until 1796. During her reign, she expanded Russia's borders, modernized the nation, and introduced various cultural projects.

- **Job:** Empress of Russia
- **Foreign Policy:** Expand Russia's Borders
- **Domestic Goals:** Westernize Russia, End Serfdom

Marble bust of Catherine the Great (1729–1796), by Jean-Antoine Houdon, 1773

Catherine the Great was born as Princess Sophie in Prussia in 1729. When Empress Elizabeth of Russia began a search for a wife for her nephew, the Grand Duke Peter, heir to the Russian throne, she invited Princess Sophie to court. She chose Sophie to be Peter's wife. In 1745, the Russian Orthodox Church rechristened Sophie as Catherine and she and Peter were married.

Peter became Czar Peter III in 1762, but he was not an effective ruler. In the nearly 20 years that she had lived in Russia, Catherine had adopted Russian customs and become popular with the Russian people. So when she wanted to overthrow her husband, the army helped her. The army arrested and assassinated Peter, and, in 1762 (the same year Peter had become czar), Catherine emerged as Russia's sole ruler.

Early in and throughout her reign, Catherine strove to change Russia's unsophisticated image. As an avid reader and student of the French Enlightenment, she admired Western culture and wished to emulate it in Russia. She built a theater for opera and ballet, collected fine works

of art, and expanded education. In addition to supporting the arts, Catherine made efforts at domestic reforms. Between 1767 and 1768, she set up a commission to codify, or systematize, Russian laws. She also tried to end serfdom. However, a rebellion made her realize that she needed the support of the nobles in order to stay in power. She responded to the rebellion by establishing local governments that increased landlords' power.

In foreign affairs, Catherine expanded Russia's borders. Wars with Turkey led to increased territory and navigation rights in Turkish waters. She wanted to gain more territory but was not able to realize her ambitions before she died in 1796.

REVIEW & ASSESS

1. **Summarize** How did Catherine the Great become Russia's sole ruler?

_____

_____

2. **Make Generalizations** What were Catherine the Great's domestic goals and did she achieve them?

_____

_____

UNIT 5 — CHAPTER 14 LESSON 2.5
Declarations of Freedom

DOCUMENT-BASED QUESTION

Use the questions here to help you analyze the sources and write your paragraph.

DOCUMENT ONE: The Declaration of Independence (1776)

1A According to the passage, what are people's "unalienable Rights"?

_____

_____

_____

_____

1B Constructed Response How did the ideas of John Locke influence the creation of the Declaration of Independence?

_____

_____

_____

DOCUMENT TWO: The Declaration of the Rights of Man and of the Citizen (1789)

2A According to the document, what are the two ways a citizen can participate in government?

_____

_____

_____

2B Constructed Response Why do you think the Declaration of the Rights of Man and of the Citizen emphasized the Enlightenment idea of equality?

_____

_____

_____

SYNTHESIZE & WRITE

What basic human rights were claimed by people following the Enlightenment?

Topic Sentence: _____

_____

Your Paragraph: _____

_____

_____

_____

_____

SOCIAL STUDIES SKILLS
READING AND WRITING

SOCIAL STUDIES SKILLS | **UNIT 1**   Chapter 1: The Roman Empire and Christianity
READING LESSON

NATIONAL GEOGRAPHIC LEARNING

SEQUENCE EVENTS

LEARNING THE STRATEGY

When you tell your friends the plot of a movie you've just seen, you probably describe its events in the order they occurred. You start at the beginning and continue to the end. When you relate events in the order in which they occurred in time, you **sequence events**. Thinking about events in time order helps you understand how they relate to each other.

Historians often sequence events to tell how a civilization developed or describe the reign of a ruler. Identifying the time order of historic events can help you understand how the events are related. Follow these steps to sequence events.

Step 1 Look for clue words and phrases that suggest time order. Clue words include the names of months and days or words such as *before, after, finally, a year later,* or *lasted.*

Step 2 Look for dates in the text and match them to events.

GUIDED MODEL

The Destruction of Pompeii

Before the afternoon of (B) August 24, A.D. 79, Pompeii was an average city resting in the shadow of Mount Vesuvius, a volcano on Italy's western coast. Some 20,000 people worked, played, ate, slept, and lived within Pompeii's city walls.

(A) And then, a violent explosion brought the city to a standstill. Mount Vesuvius erupted, shooting gas mixed with rock and ash high into the sky and creating an immense black cloud that blocked out the sun. Panic-stricken citizens fled as ash rained down.

As lava crept toward the city, fires raged and buildings collapsed. A vast volcanic ash cloud swept in to suffocate the city, burying its people and their possessions nearly 25 feet deep. A cloud of poisonous gas overtook and killed anyone who had not yet escaped. (A) Over the next few days, lightning, earthquakes, and tidal waves followed. (A) Finally after three days, Vesuvius went quiet—as silent as the deserted city of Pompeii.

Step 1 Look for clue words and phrases that suggest time order.

   Time Clues (A) and then; over the next few days; finally

Step 2 Look for specific dates in the text.

   Be sure to read the text carefully. Historians may not always list the dates in time order. As you read, it is important to match the event with its date.

   Sample Date (B) August 24, A.D. 79, when Mount Vesuvius erupted and destroyed Pompeii

TIP As you read, you can create a time line to track the time order of the events discussed in the text. A time line is a visual tool that is used to sequence events. Time lines often read from left to right, listing events from the earliest to the latest.

SOCIAL STUDIES SKILLS Continued

NATIONAL
GEOGRAPHIC
LEARNING

APPLYING THE STRATEGY

GETTING STARTED Now sequence events as you read Lesson 2.4, "The Early Christian Church," in Chapter 1. Sequencing events will help you better understand the development of the early Christian Church. As you read the lesson, use the graphic organizer below to sequence events. List the earliest event in the first box on the left and the latest event in the last box on the right. Remember to use both clue words and dates to determine the time order of events. The first box is filled in to help you get started.

COOPERATIVE OPTION You may wish to work with a partner in your class to review the lesson and complete the graphic organizer.

TAKING NOTES

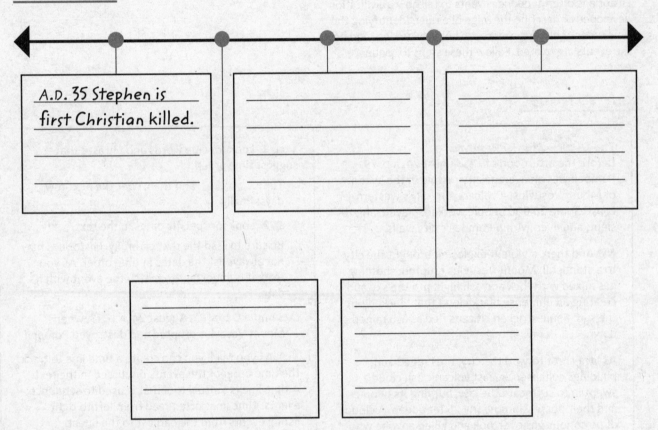

A.D. 35 Stephen is first Christian killed.

THINK AND DISCUSS

THINK ABOUT AND DISCUSS THESE QUESTIONS:

1. What event led to the deaths of thousands of Christians in Rome? When did this event occur?

2. Who ended Christian persecution, and when did this happen?

3. Put these events in chronological order: Christianity becomes Rome's official religion; the apostle Peter dies; Christian leaders meet to define Christian beliefs.

SOCIAL STUDIES SKILLS | UNIT 1

Chapter 1: The Roman Empire and Christianity
WRITING LESSON

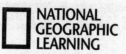

WRITE AN EXPLANATION

LEARNING THE STRATEGY

When you write an **explanation**, you give readers information about a topic. You provide facts and examples so they will understand the topic more fully. To write an explanation, first select a topic. Write a sentence that introduces and states your topic. This is your main idea. Then gather information and provide details to support your what you find. The most common types of supporting details are facts, examples, statistics, quotations, expert opinions, and personal experience.

After you select the details you want to provide on your topic, you need to arrange them in a logical order. You may present your details chronologically, sequentially, or by category.

To write an explanation, follow these steps.

Step 1 Select a topic you would like to inform your readers about and gather detailed information about it.

Step 2 Write a sentence that introduces and states your topic. This is your main idea.

Step 3 Include at least three details that provide information on your topic.

Step 4 Organize your details either chronologically, step-by-step, or by category.

Step 5 Write a concluding sentence about your topic that restates the main idea in a different way.

GUIDED MODEL

(A) Augustus and the Pax Romana
(B) When Augustus became the sole ruler of Rome, he made wise decisions that formed the foundation for the Pax Romana. **(C)** For example, Augustus helped prevent unrest within the empire by guaranteeing free grain to the poor. He also began a cultural revival in the city of Rome and encouraged Romans to pursue art, literature, and education. By making Rome more beautiful, Augustus encouraged Romans to take greater pride in their capital.

(D) Augustus also reformed the military. He decreased the size of the military and granted land to any soldiers who lost their jobs. By establishing these reforms, Augustus removed the army as a threat to his power and created a more stable government. **(E)** The decisions Augustus made while emperor of Rome contributed greatly to the peace and prosperity that Romans enjoyed during and after his rule.

Step 1 Select a topic.
  (A) The topic is Augustus and the Pax Romana.

Step 2 Write a sentence that introduces and states your topic.
  (B) This sentence states the topic.

Step 3 Include at least three details that provide information on your topic.
  (C) The writer includes details on the topic.

Step 4 Organize your details.
  (D) The writer organizes the details by category.

Step 5 Write a concluding sentence.
  (E) The writer concludes by stating the main idea again but in a different way.

TIP Use a graphic organizer to list your topic, introduction, ideas, details, and conclusion. You can use the graphic as a road map for your explanatory text.

SOCIAL STUDIES SKILLS Continued

APPLYING THE STRATEGY

GETTING STARTED Now write your own explanation. In the "Write About History" section of the Chapter Review, you are asked to write a speech that explains three of the problems that contributed to the decline and fall of the Roman Empire. Use the steps explained in this lesson and the graphic organizer below to plan your speech. The graphic will help you clearly state your topic and organize facts about your topic into different categories. After you have organized your information, write your draft.

COOPERATIVE OPTION After you have written your draft, show it to a partner in your class and invite his or her suggestions on ways to improve the draft. You can also offer suggestions for your partner's draft. Remember to be positive and constructive.

TAKING NOTES

TOPIC:

INTRODUCTION:

FACTS:

DETAILS:

CONCLUSION:

THINK AND DISCUSS

AFTER YOU HAVE FINISHED WRITING YOUR SPEECH, THINK ABOUT AND DISCUSS THESE QUESTIONS:

1. What was the greatest challenge you faced as you wrote your speech?

2. What do you consider to be the most important reason for the decline and fall of Rome? What evidence from the text makes you think so?

3. What new understanding about the decline and fall of Rome did you gain by writing your speech?

SOCIAL STUDIES SKILLS | **UNIT 1**

Chapter 2: The Byzantine Empire
READING LESSON

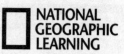

ANALYZE CAUSE AND EFFECT

LEARNING THE STRATEGY

Have you ever told a story about something that happened to you? In many stories, there's an event or action that causes something else to happen. For instance, you might say, "Because the road was slippery, our car slid into a ditch." A **cause** is an event or action that makes something else happen. An **effect** is an event that happens as a result of a cause. In this example, the cause is the slippery road; the effect is sliding into a ditch.

Historians analyze cause-and-effect relationships to figure out why events happened. They consider how an event led to changes over time. One cause can create several effects, or one effect may have more than one cause. A cause may be an event or an action. It may also be a condition, or a state of being. Follow these steps to figure out cause-and-effect relationships.

Step 1 Determine the cause(s) of an event. Look for signal words, such as *because, due to, since, so,* and *therefore.*

Step 2 Determine the effect(s) of an event. Look for signal words such as *led to, consequently,* and *as a result.*

GUIDED MODEL

The City of Constantinople
(A) Due to its strategic location on the Bosporus, **(B)** Constantinople was the richest and most influential city of its time. **(B)** Merchants and traders from many parts of Europe and Asia brought in a constant flow of business and goods. **(A)** Because it was a center of trade, **(B)** Constantinople was also a center of cultural diversity. People who came from abroad to trade sometimes settled in the city.

In spite of the city's wealth, **(A)** many of Constantinople's residents lived in poor conditions. **(B)** As a result, they relied on government handouts of bread. Just a short walk away, though, spectacular public buildings and magnificent monuments inspired civic pride.

Step 1 Determine the cause(s).

   (A) CAUSE Constantinople was strategically located on the Bosporus.

   (A) CAUSE Constantinople was a center of trade.

   (A) CAUSE Many of Constantinople's residents lived in poor conditions.

Step 2 Determine the effect(s) of an event.

   (B) EFFECT Constantinople was a rich and influential city.

   (B) EFFECT Merchants and traders brought a constant flow of business and goods.

   (B) EFFECT Constantinople was a center of cultural diversity.

   (B) EFFECT Many residents relied on government handouts of bread.

TIP Test whether events have a cause-and-effect relationship by using this construction: "Because [insert cause], [insert effect] happened." If the construction does not work, one event did not lead to the other.

SOCIAL STUDIES SKILLS Continued

NATIONAL GEOGRAPHIC LEARNING

APPLYING THE STRATEGY

GETTING STARTED Now practice analyzing cause and effect in Lesson 2.1, "The Church Divides," in Chapter 2. By examining the causes and effects of the East-West Schism, you will come to a greater understanding of this event. Use the graphic organizer below to take notes on causes and effects in the text. Recall that each cause you find may have more than one effect. To help get you started, one cause and one effect have been filled in for you.

COOPERATIVE OPTION Fill out your cause-and-effect chart and then exchange charts with a partner to compare answers. Discuss any differences you may have.

TAKING NOTES

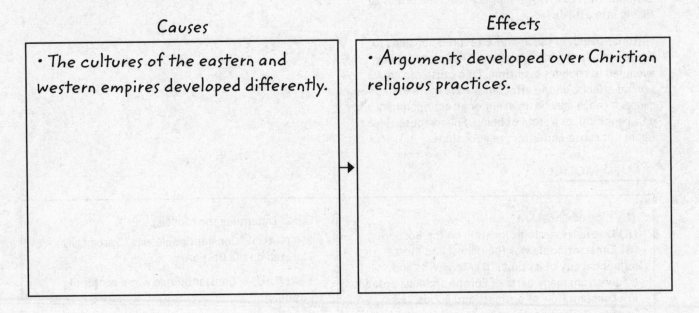

Causes

- The cultures of the eastern and western empires developed differently.

Effects

- Arguments developed over Christian religious practices.

THINK AND DISCUSS

THINK ABOUT AND DISCUSS THESE QUESTIONS:

1. What caused a power struggle between the pope in Rome and Byzantine emperors?

2. Why did the Byzantine patriarch excommunicate the pope?

3. How does examining the causes and effects of the East-West Schism help you understanding this event?

WORLD HISTORY **2 of 4**

SOCIAL STUDIES SKILLS · UNIT 1

Chapter 2: The Byzantine Empire
WRITING LESSON

NATIONAL GEOGRAPHIC LEARNING

WRITE AN EXPLANATION

LEARNING THE STRATEGY

When you write an **explanation**, you give readers information about a topic. You provide facts and examples so they will understand the topic more fully. Types of explanatory writing include newspaper articles, textbooks, encyclopedia entries, and how-to-articles.

To write an explanation, first select a topic. For example, suppose you wanted to write about Byzantine mosaics. You'd start by writing a sentence that introduces the topic. This is your main idea. Then you would include details that support your main idea. Next you would consider how best to organize your details. Last, you would conclude with a sentence that restates the main idea.

To write an explanation, follow these steps.

Step 1 Select a topic you would like to inform your readers about and gather detailed information about it.

Step 2 Write a sentence that introduces and states your topic. This is your main idea.

Step 3 Include at least three details that provide information on your topic.

Step 4 Write a concluding sentence about your topic that restates the main idea in a different way.

GUIDED MODEL

(A) BYZANTINE MOSAICS
(B) The Byzantine Empire developed an influential artistic culture, and its distinctive style is well represented by remarkable mosaics. Byzantine mosaics depicted vibrant, detailed scenes that covered entire walls and ceilings.

(C) To make a mosaic, an artist would spread a layer of plaster onto a surface and set the cubes of stone into the wet plaster. Then to create a sparkling effect, some mosaic pieces were made of gold leaf sandwiched in clear glass. **(C)** These pieces were angled precisely to reflect light in different directions. **(C)** Finally, to create highly detailed and realistic pictures of people and animals, Byzantine mosaic artists used many different colors of stone.

(D) Byzantine mosaics stood out for their exceptional quality and craftsmanship. The breathtaking results still awe viewers today.

Step 1 Select a topic.
  (A) The topic is Byzantine mosaics.

Step 2 Write a sentence that introduces and states your topic.
  (B) This sentence states the topic.

Step 3 Include at least three details that provide information on your topic.
  (C) The writer includes details on the topic.

Step 4 Write a conclusion.
  (D) The writer concludes by stating the main idea again but in a different way.

TIP Think about the best way to organize your details for your readers. Determine what makes the most sense for your topic. You could organize information chronologically, in numbered steps, or in categories.

SOCIAL STUDIES SKILLS Continued

NATIONAL GEOGRAPHIC LEARNING

APPLYING THE STRATEGY

GETTING STARTED Now write your own explanation. In the "Write About History" section of the Chapter Review, you are asked to suppose you are a citizen of the Byzantine Empire and write an explanation to your fellow citizens about how Theodora influenced Justinian's rule. Use the steps explained in this lesson and the graphic organizer below to plan your writing. Begin by filling in your main idea. Then come up with three details that explain the ways in which Theodora influenced Justinian's rule. After you have organized your information, write your draft.

COOPERATIVE OPTION After you have written a first draft, show it to a partner in your class and invite his or her suggestions to improve the draft. You can also offer suggestions for your partner's first draft. Remember to be positive and constructive.

TAKING NOTES

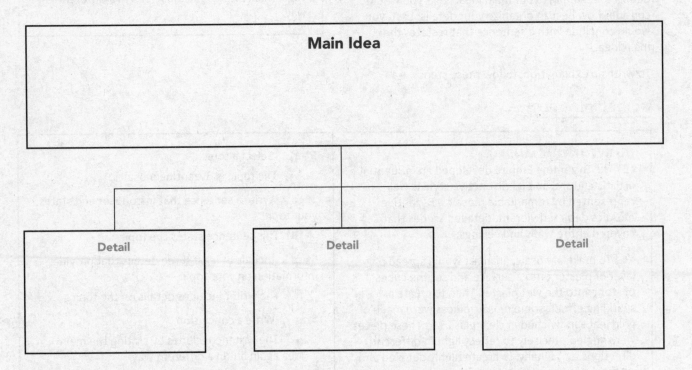

Main Idea

Detail   Detail   Detail

THINK AND DISCUSS

AFTER YOU HAVE FINISHED WRITING YOUR EXPLANATION, THINK ABOUT AND DISCUSS THESE QUESTIONS:

1. What do you think is the most important way in which Theodora influenced Justinian?

2. What challenges did you face while writing your explanation?

3. What understanding about Theodora and Justinian's relationship did you gain by writing the explanation?

SOCIAL STUDIES SKILLS UNIT 1

Chapter 3: The Islamic World
READING LESSON

NATIONAL GEOGRAPHIC LEARNING

IDENTIFY MAIN IDEAS AND DETAILS

LEARNING THE STRATEGY

Have you ever tried to describe a movie to someone? If you recited every detail, your friend would probably get bored pretty quickly. Instead, you should figure out what's most important and just tell your friend that. Once your friend grasps the main idea, you should supply a few important ideas to support it.

Main ideas are in everything you read: paragraphs, passages, chapters, and books. The **main idea** is the most important idea in a text. Sometimes the main idea is a sentence or sentences, but other times it may just be implied. The **supporting details** are the facts that support the main idea. If the main idea is implied, the supporting details provide clues about the main idea. To find the main idea and details of a paragraph, follow these steps.

Step 1 Look for the main idea by reading the first and last sentences in the introductory paragraph. If the main idea is not directly stated, look for details that give you clues about the main idea.

Step 2 Identify details that tell more about the main idea. They may be facts, examples, or quotations, or other specific items that clarify the main idea. If the main idea is in the first sentence, the supporting details follow it. If the main idea is stated in the last sentence, the supporting details come before it.

GUIDED MODEL

Minarets in Islamic Architecture
Minarets are a distinctive architectural feature of mosques. However, the earliest mosques lacked these tall, thin towers. **(A)** Historians disagree about how minarets originated.

(B) Some historians believe that minarets originated during the Umayyad dynasty in Syria. **(B)** They believe that Muslims saw church towers or steeples and built similar structures from which Muslims could be called to prayer.

(B) Others claim that minarets were based on temples known as ziggurats in Babylonia and Assyria. A ziggurat is a rectangular, tiered tower. Some ziggurats had stairs that wound around the outside walls. At least one early minaret (on the Great Mosque of Samarra in present-day Iraq) also had stairs that wound around the outside. **(B)** Although the minaret is round, not rectangular, some historians believe it may have been inspired by ziggurats.

Step 1 Find the main idea in the first paragraph.

  (A) MAIN IDEA Historians disagree about how minarets originated.

Step 2 Find the supporting details in the rest of the passage.

  (B) DETAIL Some historians believe that minarets originated during the Umayyad dynasty in Syria.

  (B) DETAIL They believe that Muslims saw church towers or steeples and built similar structures from which Muslims could be called to prayer.

  (B) DETAIL Others claim that minarets were based on temples known as ziggurats in Babylonia and Assyria.

  (B) DETAIL Although the minaret is round, not rectangular, some historians believe it may have been inspired by ziggurats.

TIP When the main idea isn't stated in the first or last sentence, you have to find the implied main idea. Look at the details in the paragraph and ask yourself what they have in common. Then find the connection between them and put it in your own words. This is the implied main idea.

SOCIAL STUDIES SKILLS Continued

APPLYING THE STRATEGY

GETTING STARTED Now identify the main idea and details in Lesson 2.4, "The Ottoman Empire," in Chapter 3. Read the section titled "A Vast Empire" and use the graphic organizer below to record its main idea in the large, center circle and the supporting details in the smaller circles. Note that the main idea of the section is implied. You will have to infer it by reading the paragraphs under the heading. To get you started, the first detail is filled in for you.

COOPERATIVE OPTION You may wish to work with a partner in your class to review the lesson and complete the graphic organizer.

TAKING NOTES

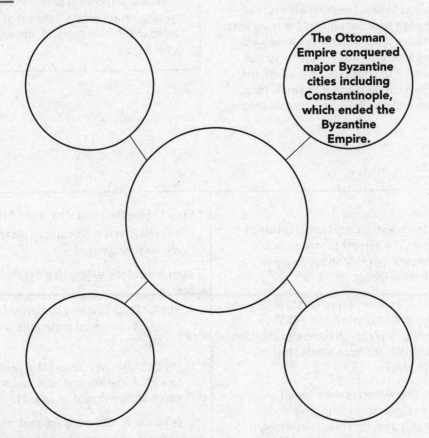

The Ottoman Empire conquered major Byzantine cities including Constantinople, which ended the Byzantine Empire.

THINK AND DISCUSS

THINK ABOUT AND DISCUSS THESE QUESTIONS:

1. What sentences in the section provide clues to the main idea?

2. What is the purpose of the details in the third paragraph, which begins with the sentence, "However, military conquest wasn't Suleyman's only interest"?

3. Why does the author give the supporting details in the order in which they are presented?

SOCIAL STUDIES SKILLS | **UNIT 1**

Chapter 3: The Islamic World
WRITING LESSON

NATIONAL GEOGRAPHIC LEARNING

WRITE AN INFORMATIVE ARTICLE

LEARNING THE STRATEGY

When you write an **informative article**, you tell readers about a topic in an objective way. In other words, you inform readers without interjecting your own opinions. Let's say you want to write an article comparing how two Muslim leaders influenced their culture. Remember that when you compare, you study similarities. You could begin by introducing the topic simply: "Both Suleyman and Akbar were interested in literature and the arts and influenced the culture of the Islamic empires they ruled." This introduction states the main idea.

Next, gather information to support your main idea. For example, you might find information about the literature or art the leaders were interested in. Finally, you would end the text with a concluding sentence that summarizes or restates the main idea in a different way.

To write an informative article, follow these steps.

Step 1 Select a topic you would like to inform your readers about and gather detailed information about it.

Step 2 Write a sentence that introduces and states your topic. This is your main idea.

Step 3 Include at least three details on your topic.

Step 4 Write a conclusion that restates the main idea in a different way.

GUIDED MODEL

(A) Culture in Muslim Empires
Suleyman I and Akbar the Great were leaders of different Islamic empires. **(B)** Both Suleyman and Akbar were interested in literature and the arts and influenced the culture of the Islamic empires they ruled.

(C) Suleyman I ruled the Ottoman Empire. **(C)** His interest in literature led him to study and write poetry. **(C)** His interest in art led him to do work as a goldsmith. **(C)** Both literature and the arts flourished under his rule.

(C) The leader of the Moghul Empire, Akbar the Great, was also devoted to literature and the arts. **(C)** He had a huge library with books in many languages. People from different cultures came to the library to study and share ideas. **(C)** He was also interested in painting. **(C)** With his support, Moghul artists created small highly detailed paintings called *miniatures*. **(D)** Thanks to both of these leaders, literature and the arts held a prominent position in Muslim culture.

Step 1: Select a topic.

   (A) The topic is culture in Muslim empires.

Step 2: Write a sentence that introduces and states the main idea.

   (B) This sentence states the main idea.

Step 3: Include at least three details on your topic. In this article, details have been chosen that can be compared.

   (C) The writer includes details on the topic and compares them.

Step 4: Write a concluding sentence.

   (D) The writer concludes by stating the main idea again but in a different way.

TIP When you research, you might gather more information than you need. Choose the information that best shows similarities.

SOCIAL STUDIES SKILLS Continued

APPLYING THE STRATEGY

GETTING STARTED Now write your own informative article. In the "Write About History" section of the Chapter Review, you are asked to write an encyclopedia article that compares the main beliefs of Islam with those of Judaism and Christianity. Use the steps explained in this lesson and the graphic organizer below to list the beliefs you are going to compare. Then write a first draft.

COOPERATIVE OPTION You may want to work in a group of three. Each group member can gather information about a different set of beliefs. Then you can work together to write a main idea and concluding statement and combine the information you gathered into one encyclopedia article.

TAKING NOTES

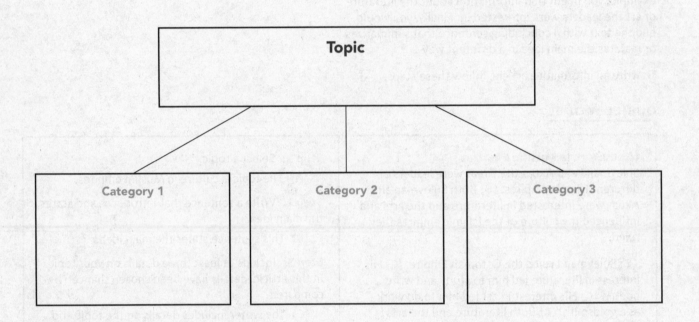

THINK AND DISCUSS

AFTER YOU HAVE FINISHED WRITING YOUR ENCYCLOPEDIA ARTICLE, THINK ABOUT AND DISCUSS THESE QUESTIONS:

1. What was one challenge you faced in writing your encyclopedia article?

2. How did you decide which details to include in your article?

3. What was the most important idea you learned about the similarities between Islam, Judaism, and Christianity from writing your encyclopedia article?

SOCIAL STUDIES SKILLS | UNIT 2

Chapter 4: North and West Africa
READING LESSON

NATIONAL GEOGRAPHIC LEARNING

ANALYZE LANGUAGE USE

LEARNING THE STRATEGY

In the same way that artists choose colors, writers choose words to communicate clearly and effectively. Carefully chosen words make text inviting, lively, and powerful. So, for example, the sentence "The shaggy-haired mutt made a made dash through the open door" is more interesting than "The dog ran through the open door."

Good readers **analyze language use** to determine the impact of the language a writer uses. They ask themselves, "Why did the writer choose this particular word?" They also use context clues to understand unfamiliar words. In addition, good readers look for suggested meanings, or connotations, of words. For example, the words *cheap* and *economical* have similar meanings, but their suggested meanings differ.

To analyze language use, follow these steps.

Step 1 Look for specific nouns, attention-getting verbs, and descriptive adjectives and adverbs.

Step 2 Identify words and phrases that have positive or negative connotations.

Step 3 Determine the impact of the language.

GUIDED MODEL

Characteristics of Camels
Early traders in the Sahara owed their livelihoods to Arabian camels. These **(A)** sturdy beasts of burden **(A)** effortlessly transported heavy loads of goods as they **(A)** trekked across the desert.

The Sahara is a **(B)** parched land with few water sources and **(B)** sparse plant life. Arabian camels have adaptations that allow them to survive in the **(B)** inhospitable desert. One adaptation is their hump, which holds large amounts of fat for later use. Camels can get water from the stored fat. This allows them to go without drinking for a week or longer.

This **(B)** unique adaptation is one reason why camels were **(B)** ideal animals to haul goods across the Sahara long ago. These "ships of the desert" allowed trade to flourish in North Africa.

Step 1 Look for specific nouns, attention-getting verbs, and descriptive adjectives and adverbs.

(A) Camels are referred to as "sturdy" animals who "effortlessly" carried loads as they "trekked" across the desert.

Step 2 Identify words and phrases that have positive or negative connotations.

(B) NEGATIVE The words *parched, sparse*, and *inhospitable* are used to describe the Sahara.

(B) POSITIVE The words *unique* and *ideal* are used to describe camels.

Step 3 Determine the impact of the language.

The language the writer uses suggests that the Sahara was a difficult place to cross for trade, but that camels were the perfects animals to haul the goods.

TIP As you read, jot down interesting or unfamiliar words to analyze later.

SOCIAL STUDIES SKILLS Continued

APPLYING THE STRATEGY

GETTING STARTED Now try analyzing language use in Lesson 1.2, "Trans-Saharan Trade," in Chapter 4. By studying word use, you will get a better sense of what life was like for early desert traders. You may even begin to feel like you were there. Use the graphic organizer below to jot down words that catch your interest, and then determine the impact of the language and what it suggests. To get you started, one example is filled in for you.

COOPERATIVE OPTION You may wish to compare your words and suggested meanings with those of three classmates.

TAKING NOTES

Language Example	What It Suggests
snakes	a long lines that curves, like the body of a snake

THINK AND DISCUSS

THINK ABOUT AND DISCUSS THESE QUESTIONS:

1. What image does the phrase *camels trudge surefooted* convey?

2. Why is *clashes* a good word to use to describe the fighting between Berbers and foreign rulers?

3. Why do you think the writer said that camels *transformed* trade in North Africa rather than just *changed* it?

SOCIAL STUDIES SKILLS | **UNIT 2**

Chapter 4: North and West Africa
WRITING LESSON

NATIONAL GEOGRAPHIC LEARNING

WRITE A NARRATIVE

LEARNING THE STRATEGY

A history text usually contains narrative accounts of events. A **narrative** is an account or story of events or experiences. Narratives may be fictional or factual. To write a historical narrative, you must understand the events, people, and places you plan to write about.

All narratives share certain characteristics, including a specific setting, or time and place. The events in a narrative usually follow a logical sequence, or order. This helps the reader understand the connections among events. Descriptive details, such as sensory details, help bring events and people to life. Sensory details are details that appeal to sight, sound, touch, taste, and smell.

Before writing a narrative, you should decide what point of view you will use. Most narratives are written from either a first-person or third-person point of view.

To write a historical narrative, follow these steps.

Step 1 Identify the topic of your narrative and gather facts about its events, people, and places.

Step 2 Determine the setting and point of view of your narrative.

Step 3 Recount events in a logical sequence.

Step 4 Use descriptive details to help bring your narrative to life.

GUIDED MODEL

(A) Taking the North African Trade Route
(B) Every day, I watched for signs of winter. "When the desert cools," Father said, "we'll head northeast to join the caravan." We are to be among the first to leave Timbuktu to cross the Sahara on the North African trade route.

(C) The day finally came, and our group set off. We had settled into a routine—eight miles each night and rest during the day—when our guide spied men on camelback in the distance. "Thieves!" he shouted. Luckily, as the villains approached, the sandstorm that had threatened all day struck in full force. We hunkered down and watched as the **(D)** stinging sand drove the men away. I was grateful when, free of storms and thieves, we resumed our routine.

After many days, date palms appeared on the horizon—the oasis! **(D)** The marketplace there shimmered with silks and gold on display. The scent of cinnamon pricked the air. But best of all, there was fresh water. I quenched my thirst and forgot about the dangers of the desert.

Step 1 Identify the topic of your narrative.

  (A) The writer is narrating what happened while taking the North African trade route.

Step 2 Determine the setting and point of view of your narrative.

  (B) The narrative is at the beginning of winter in Timbuktu. It is around A.D. 800, the time when the North and West African trade routes across the Sahara opened up. The writer uses the pronouns *I* and *we* and so is employing a first-person point of view.

Step 3 Recount events in a logical sequence.

  (C) The writer takes readers through the journey in a logical sequence.

Step 4 Use descriptive details to help bring your narrative to life.

  (D) The writer uses sensory details to describe the sandstorm and how the marketplace looked and smelled.

TIP Use an outline to help you organize the events of your narrative and write them in a logical order.

SOCIAL STUDIES SKILLS Continued

APPLYING THE STRATEGY

GETTING STARTED Now write your own narrative. In the "Write About History" section of the Chapter Review, you are asked to take on the role of a traveler to the trading city of Timbuktu and describe what happens during that time and what you see there. Use the steps explained in this lesson and the graphic organizer below to develop your narrative. Begin by creating an outline to plan your narrative. Write down key ideas after the roman numerals in the outline. Write down details after the letters in the outline. Be sure to choose descriptive details that help bring your narrative to life. Follow your outline as you draft your narrative.

COOPERATIVE OPTION After you have written your draft, show it to a partner in your class and invite his or her suggestions on ways to improve the draft. You can also offer suggestions for your partner's draft. Remember to be positive and constructive.

TAKING NOTES

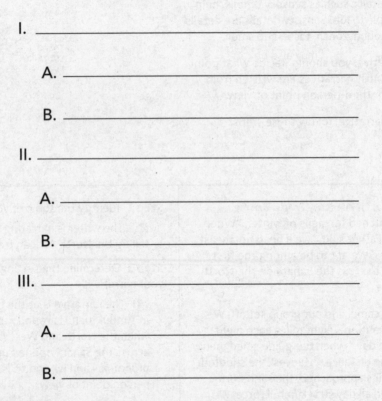

I. _____

    A. _____

    B. _____

II. _____

    A. _____

    B. _____

III. _____

    A. _____

    B. _____

THINK AND DISCUSS

AFTER YOU HAVE FINISHED WRITING YOUR NARRATIVE, THINK ABOUT AND DISCUSS THESE QUESTIONS:

1. What part of this writing assignment did you find easiest? What part was hardest?

2. What methods did you use to attract and maintain the interest of readers?

3. Why did you choose your ending to the story rather than another possible ending?

SOCIAL STUDIES SKILLS | UNIT 2
Chapter 5: East, Central, and Southern Africa
READING LESSON

NATIONAL GEOGRAPHIC LEARNING

ANALYZE CAUSE AND EFFECT

LEARNING THE STRATEGY

Think about what happens when you bounce a ball. First, you push the ball toward the ground. The ball moves downward, strikes the ground, and then bounces back up. This series of events shows **cause and effect**. Pushing the ball is a **cause**. A cause is an event, action, or condition that makes something else happen. The action of pushing the ball causes several **effects**. An effect is an event that results from a cause.

Historians analyze cause and effect to figure out why events happened. They consider how an event led to changes over time. One cause can create several effects, or one effect may have more than one cause. A cause may be an event or an action. It may also be a condition, or a state of being. Follow these steps to figure out cause-and-effect relationships.

Step 1 Determine the cause of an event or action. Look for signal words such as *because*, *since*, *due to*, and *therefore*.

Step 2 Determine the effect that results from the cause. Look for signal words such as *led to*, *consequently*, and *as a result*.

Step 3 Look for a chain of causes and effects. An effect may be the cause of another action or event.

GUIDED MODEL

The Rise and Fall of Prosperity in Aksum
The Red Sea connects East Africa with the Persian Gulf, the Mediterranean Sea, and the Indian Ocean. **(A)** Because of Aksum's location in East Africa, **(B)** it became a major international trading hub.

(A) Aksum's economy grew through the trade of ivory, spices, and slaves. **(B)** This economic growth also led to cultural achievements such as the production of luxury goods by artisans and the development of a written language that was used to create a rich body of literature.

This time of prosperity in Aksum did not last. **(C)** Beginning in the A.D. 500s, there were regional wars and Arab expansion in the area. As a result, Aksum's key trade routes were closed off. Aksum declined, and Muslim invaders shrank its borders.

Step 1 Determine the cause.
 (A) CAUSE Aksum was well located in East Africa near the Red Sea.
 (A) CAUSE Aksum's economy grew through the trade of ivory, spices, and slaves.

Step 2 Determine the effect.
 (B) EFFECT Aksum became a major international trading hub.
 (B) EFFECT Economic growth in Aksum brought about cultural achievements.

Step 3 Look for a chain of causes and effects.
 (C) CAUSE/EFFECTS In the A.D. 500s, there were regional wars and Arab expansion in Aksum. As a result, trade routes were closed off, Aksum declined, and Muslim invaders shrank its borders.

TIP Test whether events have a cause-and-effect relationship by using this construction: "Because [insert cause], [insert effect] happened." If the construction does not work, one event did not lead to the other.

© National Geographic Learning, Cengage Learning

SOCIAL STUDIES SKILLS Continued

APPLYING THE STRATEGY

GETTING STARTED Now practice analyzing cause and effect in Lesson 1.2, "Indian Ocean Trade" in Chapter 5. Use your analysis of cause and effect to develop a better understanding of what happened as a result of the expansion of trade along the Indian Ocean. Use the graphic organizer below to list the effects of the expansion of Indian Ocean trade. Remember to look for signal words to help identify effects.

COOPERATIVE OPTION Fill out your cause-and-effect chart and then exchange charts with a partner to compare answers. Discuss any differences you may have.

TAKING NOTES

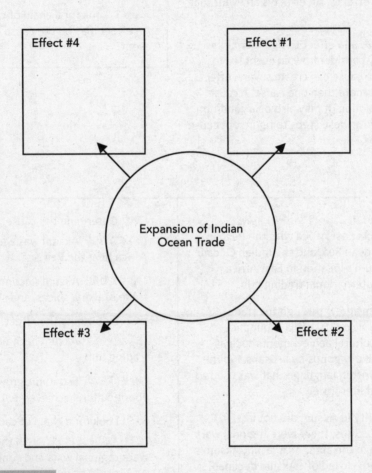

THINK AND DISCUSS

THINK ABOUT AND DISCUSS THESE QUESTIONS:

1. What did East African mariners do that led to the expansion of trade across the Indian Ocean?

2. How did the expansion of Indian Ocean trade affect settlements along East Africa's coast?

3. How did the expansion of Indian Ocean trade affect religion in East Africa?

SOCIAL STUDIES SKILLS | UNIT 2 — Chapter 5: East, Central, and Southern Africa — WRITING LESSON

NATIONAL GEOGRAPHIC LEARNING

WRITE AN INFORMATIVE OUTLINE

LEARNING THE STRATEGY

When you write an informative text, you tell readers about a topic in an objective and factual way. One type of informative writing is an **outline**. You can use an outline to organize and summarize the ideas in a text to help you understand important information. You can also write an outline to help you plan a piece of writing, either chronologically or by level of importance.

A good outline lists the most important ideas and supporting details in an organized way. An outline has a basic structure. Write the title, which states the topic, at the top of the outline. Use Roman numerals for the main ideas and capital letters for the sub-points that explain the main ideas.

To write an outline, follow these steps.

> **Step 1** Give your outline a title.
>
> **Step 2** Determine and record the main ideas in logical order using Roman numerals.
>
> **Step 3** Determine and record specific details below the appropriate main ideas using capital letters.

GUIDED MODEL

(A) Arab Influence in East Africa

(B) I. Arab merchants settled in East African towns.

(C)   A. They brought Islam to East Africa.

        B. They married into local families.

        C. They began to control trade in East Africa.

    II. East African and Arabic Muslim culture combined to form the Swahili culture.

        A. The Swahili language became the language of trade and the common language of all East Africans.

        B. Islam became widespread, which, in addition to the common language, helped unify the East African people.

Step 1 Give your outline a title.
  (A) The topic is the title of the outline.

Step 2 Determine and record the main ideas in a logical order using Roman numerals.
  (B) The main ideas are listed using Roman numerals. The main ideas are causes.

Step 3 Determine and record specific details below the appropriate main ideas using capital letters.
  (C) Details are listed using capital letters. The details are effects.

TIP You may want to list causes and effects in a graphic organizer. Then, use the causes and effects you listed to help you determine an appropriate organization for your outline.

SOCIAL STUDIES SKILLS Continued

APPLYING THE STRATEGY

GETTING STARTED Now write your own informative outline. In the "Write About History" section of the Chapter Review, you are asked to write an outline of the causes and effects of the slave trade between the kingdom of Kongo and Portugal. Use the steps explained in this lesson and the graphic organizer below to plan your outline. Write causes in the left column and effects in the right column. Then use this information to write your outline.

COOPERATIVE OPTION After you have written your outline, show it to a classmate and invite him or her to provide suggestions to improve it. You can also offer suggestions for your partner's outline. Remember to be positive and constructive.

TAKING NOTES

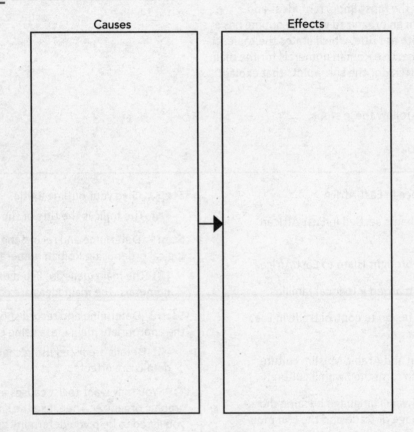

Causes   Effects

THINK AND DISCUSS

AFTER YOU HAVE FINISHED WRITING YOUR INFORMATIVE OUTLINE, THINK ABOUT AND DISCUSS THESE QUESTIONS:

1. What was one challenge you faced when gathering information for your outline?

2. What did you find most interesting about the roles that the kingdom of Kongo and Portugal played in the development of slavery?

3. What understanding about the relationship between the kingdom of Kongo and Portugal did you gain by writing your outline?

SOCIAL STUDIES SKILLS | UNIT 3

Chapter 6: Mesoamerica
READING LESSON

IDENTIFY MAIN IDEAS AND DETAILS

LEARNING THE STRATEGY

Have you ever watched a movie or read a book and then tried to tell a friend about it? If you recited every detail, your friend would probably get bored pretty quickly. Instead, you should figure out what's most important and tell that to your friend. Once your friend grasps the main idea, you can supply a few important details about the main idea.

Main ideas are in everything you read: paragraphs, passages, chapters, and books. The **main idea** is the most important idea in a text. Sometimes the main idea is a sentence or sentences, but other times it may just be implied. The **supporting details** are the facts that support the main idea. If the main idea is implied, the supporting details provide clues about the main idea. Being able to identify a main idea and its supporting details will help you understand a text more fully. To find the main idea and details of a paragraph, follow these steps.

Step 1 Look for the main idea in the first and last sentences of a paragraph. If the main idea is not clearly stated, look for details that give you clues about what the main idea is.

Step 2 Find the supporting details in the paragraph. These are facts, statistics, ideas, examples, quotations, and other specific items that clarify the main idea. If the main idea is in the first sentence, the supporting details follow it. If the main idea is stated in the last sentence, the supporting details come before it.

GUIDED MODEL

Maya Class System
(A) The development of Maya cities produced a class system with four main classes. **(B)** At the top was the king, who performed religious ceremonies and was believed to have descended from the gods. **(B)** Next came priests and warriors. The priests decided when farmers could plant and when people could marry. They also conducted important religious rituals and ceremonies. **(B)** Merchants and craftspeople followed the upper classes. Craftspeople made articles out of pottery and designed buildings and temples. The merchants sold and traded goods. **(B)** Finally, farmers, who made up the majority of the population, and slaves were at the bottom of the heap.

Step 1 Find the main idea in the first or last sentence.

  (A) MAIN IDEA: The development of Maya cities produced a class system with four main classes.

Step 2 Find the supporting details in the paragraph.

  (B) DETAIL: At the top was the king.

  (B) DETAIL: Next came priests and warriors.

  (B) DETAIL: Merchants and craftspeople followed the upper classes.

  (B) DETAIL: Farmers and slaves were at the bottom of the heap.

Tip When the main idea isn't stated in the first or last sentence, you have to find the implied main idea. Look at the details in the paragraph and ask yourself what they have in common. Then find the connection between them and put it in your own words. This is the implied main idea.

195

SOCIAL STUDIES SKILLS Continued

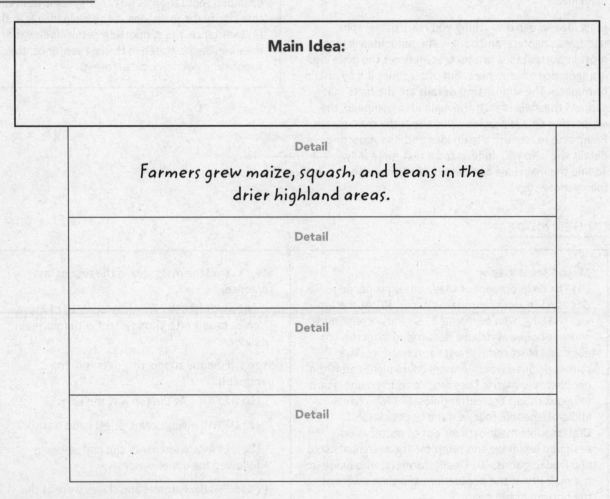

APPLYING THE STRATEGY

GETTING STARTED Now identify the main idea and the supporting details in Lesson 1.1, "The Geography of Mesoamerica," in Chapter 6. Read the first paragraph under "Agriculture" and use the graphic organizer below to record its main idea and supporting details. This will help you gain a deeper understanding of Mesoamerican farmers, their landscape, and the crops they grew. To get you started, one supporting detail is filled in.

COOPERATIVE OPTION You may wish to work with a partner in your class to review the lesson and complete the graphic organizer.

TAKING NOTES

Main Idea:

Detail

Farmers grew maize, squash, and beans in the drier highland areas.

Detail

Detail

Detail

THINK AND DISCUSS

THINK ABOUT AND DISCUSS THESE QUESTIONS:

1. Where did you find the main idea in this paragraph?

2. Where did you find the supporting details in the paragraph?

3. How do the details in the paragraph support the main idea?

SOCIAL STUDIES SKILLS | UNIT 3

Chapter 6: Mesoamerica
WRITING LESSON

NATIONAL GEOGRAPHIC LEARNING

WRITE AN EXPLANATION

LEARNING THE STRATEGY

When you write an **explanation**, you give readers information about a topic. You provide facts and examples so they will understand the topic more fully. Types of explanatory writing include newspaper articles, textbooks, encyclopedia entries, and how-to articles.

To write an explanation, first select a topic. For example, suppose you want to write about the Zapotec people. You'd start by writing a sentence that introduces the topic. This is your main idea. Then you would include details that support your main idea. Next you would consider how best to organize your details. Last, you would conclude with a sentence that restates the main idea.

To write an explanation, follow these steps.

Step 1 Select a topic you would like to inform your readers about and gather detailed information about it.

Step 2 Write a sentence that introduces and states your topic. This is your main idea.

Step 3 Include at least three details that provide information on your topic.

Step 4 Organize your details either chronologically, step-by-step, or by category.

Step 5 Write a concluding sentence about your topic that restates the main idea in a different way.

GUIDED MODEL

(A) The Zapotec
(B) The Zapotec developed their own distinct and powerful civilization. **(C)** The Zapotec people would build one of the first major cities in Mesoamerica. **(C)** They developed their society in the Oaxaca Valley, a large, open area where three smaller valleys meet. **(C)** This fertile area, with its river, mild climate, and abundant rainfall, proved excellent for growing crops, especially maize. **(C)** For centuries, the Zapotec lived in farming villages located throughout the Oaxaca Valley. **(D)** Then, around 1300 B.C., a settlement called San José Magote emerged as the Zapotec center of power. Around 500 B.C., the center of power shifted when the Zapotec built a city known now as Monte Albán high atop a mountain. In time, nearly half of the Zapotec people lived in San José Magote. **(E)** With its great plazas, pyramids, and palaces, Monte Albán became the first true urban center in the Americas and a fitting symbol of the mighty Zapotec civilization.

Step 1 Select a topic.
  (A) The topic is the Zapotec.

Step 2 Write a sentence that introduces and states your topic.
  (B) This sentence states the topic.

Step 3 Include at least three details that provide information on your topic.
  (C) The writer includes details on the topic.

Step 4 Organize your details.
  (D) The writer organizes the details chronologically.

Step 5 Write a concluding sentence.
  (E) The writer concludes by stating the main idea again but in a different way.

TIP Before writing, record notes on your topic in a graphic organizer. Then select the facts, details, and examples that best develop your topic.

SOCIAL STUDIES SKILLS Continued

APPLYING THE STRATEGY

GETTING STARTED Now write your own explanation. In the "Write About History" section of the Chapter Review, you are asked to write a paragraph that explains the similarities and differences among Mesoamerican civilizations. Use the steps explained in this lesson and the graphic organizer below to plan your explanation. The graphic will help you organize similarities and differences. After you have organized your information, write your draft.

COOPERATIVE OPTION After you have written your draft, show it to a partner in your class and invite his or her suggestions on ways to improve the draft. You can also offer suggestions for your partner's draft. Remember to be positive and constructive.

TAKING NOTES

Civilizations	Similarities	Differences
Olmec		
Zapotec		
Maya		
Aztec		

THINK AND DISCUSS

AFTER YOU HAVE FINISHED WRITING YOUR EXPLANATION, THINK ABOUT AND DISCUSS THESE QUESTIONS:

1. What was one challenge you faced when writing your explanation?

2. What do you consider to be the most important similarity or difference among the Mesoamerican civilizations? What evidence from the text makes you think so?

3. What new understanding about Mesoamerican civilizations did you gain by writing your explanatory paragraph?

SOCIAL STUDIES SKILLS | UNIT 3

Chapter 7: South and North America
READING LESSON

NATIONAL GEOGRAPHIC LEARNING

SEQUENCE EVENTS

LEARNING THE STRATEGY

Suppose a friend asks what you did on the weekend. You might describe the events in the order they occurred, beginning with Friday evening and continuing to Sunday night. When you relate events in the order in which they occurred in time, you **sequence events**. Thinking about events in time order helps you understand how they relate to each other.

Historians often sequence events to tell how a civilization developed or describe the reign of a ruler. Identifying the time order of historic events can help you understand how the events are related. Follow these steps to sequence events.

Step 1 Look for clue words and phrases that suggest time order. Clue words include the names of months and days or words such as *before, after, finally, a year later,* or *lasted.*

Step 2 Look for dates in the text and match them to events.

GUIDED MODEL

The Cherokee: Changes in the 1800s
The Cherokee faced many changes **(B)** during the 1800s. **(A)** By the beginning of the century, they had already adapted to many of the American settlers' ways of life. As a result, a Cherokee named Sequoyah feared that his people's culture would be lost forever. So in **(B)** 1821, he created a writing system for the Cherokee language. **(A)** In the years that followed, the Cherokee used the system to record their history.

(A) At about this time, more settlers entered the land on which the Cherokee lived. **(A)** Soon it became clear that the settlers wanted the land for themselves. Then in **(B)** 1830, President Andrew Jackson approved the Indian Removal Act. At first, the Cherokee protested. They even took the matter to the Supreme Court. But in **(B)** 1838, the U.S. government began forcing the Cherokee to move to what is now Oklahoma. Their journey is known as the Trail of Tears.

Step 1 Look for clue words and phrases that suggest time order.

  Time Clues (A) by the beginning of the century; in the years that followed; at about this time; soon it became clear

Step 2 Look for specific dates in the text.

The dates in this model are given in the order in which they occurred, but be sure to read all texts carefully. Historians may not always list the dates in time order. You may have to match the event with its date.

  Sample Date (B) during the 1800s, when the Cherokee faced many changes

Tip As you read, you can create a time line to track the time order of the events discussed in the text. A time line is a visual tool that is used to sequence events. Time lines often read from left to right, listing events from the earliest to the latest.

SOCIAL STUDIES SKILLS Continued

APPLYING THE STRATEGY

GETTING STARTED Now sequence events as you read Lesson 2.2, "The Ancient Pueblo," in Chapter 7. Sequencing events will help you better understand the history of the ancient Pueblo. As you read the lesson, use the graphic organizer below to sequence events. List the earliest event in the first box on the left and the latest event in the last box on the right. Remember to use both clue words and dates to determine the time order of events. The first box is filled in to help you get started.

COOPERATIVE OPTION You may wish to work with a partner in your class to review the lesson and complete the graphic organizer.

TAKING NOTES

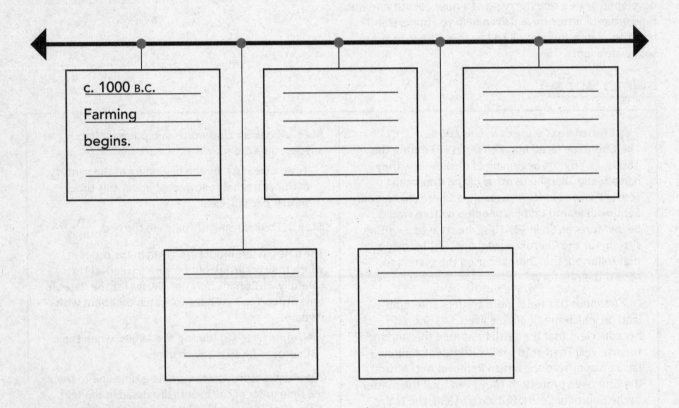

c. 1000 B.C.
Farming
begins.

THINK AND DISCUSS

THINK ABOUT AND DISCUSS THESE QUESTIONS:

1. About how long is the period of time described in this lesson?

2. What types of clues helped you most in identifying the sequence of events related to the ancient Pueblo?

3. About what year did construction of Pueblo Bonito end? How did you determine this?

SOCIAL STUDIES SKILLS | **UNIT 3**

Chapter 7: South and North America
WRITING LESSON

NATIONAL GEOGRAPHIC LEARNING

WRITE AN INFORMATIVE PARAGRAPH

LEARNING THE STRATEGY

When you write an **informative paragraph**, you tell readers about a topic in an objective way. In other words, you inform readers without interjecting your own opinions. Suppose you want to write an informative paragraph about early agricultural methods in the Americas. You could begin by introducing the topic: "Despite challenging environments, early native people of the Americas found ways to grow crops." This introduction states the main idea.

Next, include more specific information to support the main idea. For example, you might add that some native people built irrigation systems. You would continue to support the main idea by providing details and examples. Finally, you would end the text with a concluding sentence that summarizes or restates the main idea in a different way.

To write an informative paragraph, follow these steps.

Step 1 Select a topic you would like to inform your readers about and gather detailed information about it.

Step 2 Write a sentence that introduces and states your topic. This is your main idea.

Step 3 Include at least three details that provide information on your topic.

Step 4 Write a conclusion that restates the main idea in a different way.

GUIDED MODEL

(A) Early Agriculture in the Americas
(B) Despite challenging environments, early native people of the Americas found ways to grow crops. **(C)** For example, the Moche lived in the desert in South America. They built irrigation systems that brought water to their arid land. This allowed them to grow corn, beans, and other crops. **(C)** The ancient Pueblo in North America also lived in an arid climate. They too built irrigation systems to water their corn, beans, and squash. **(C)** The Inca lived high up in the Andes Mountains. They planted crops on terraces that they built into the steep mountainsides. Plants that grew on the terraces did not wash away. The terraces also served to trap water for the crops. **(D)** Cultures throughout the Americas found innovative ways to grow food.

Step 1 Select a topic.

  (A) The topic is early agriculture in the Americas.

Step 2 Write a sentence that introduces and states the main idea.

  (B) This sentence states the main idea.

Step 3 Include at least three details that provide information on your topic.

  (C) The writer includes details on the topic.

Step 4 Write a concluding sentence.

  (D) The writer concludes by stating the main idea again but in a different way.

TIP Gather as many details as you can and list them in a Main Idea and Details chart. Then number the details in the order that you think will be the most effective.

SOCIAL STUDIES SKILLS Continued

NATIONAL GEOGRAPHIC LEARNING

APPLYING THE STRATEGY

GETTING STARTED Now write your own informative paragraph. In the "Write About History" section of the Chapter Review, you are asked to write a paragraph for a booklet about Native American cultures. The paragraph should be about the impact of the Spanish use of guns and horses on either the Inca or the people of the Great Plains. Use the steps explained in this lesson and the graphic organizer below to plan your informative paragraph. The graphic organizer will help you organize your main idea and details. After you have determined your main idea and details, write your draft.

COOPERATIVE OPTION Work with a partner in your class who has selected the same Native American group. Together, brainstorm supporting details related to the introduction of guns and horses. Then work together to write your informative paragraph.

TAKING NOTES

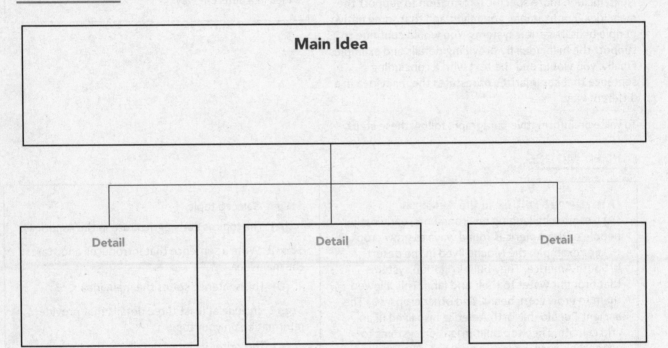

Main Idea

Detail   Detail   Detail

THINK AND DISCUSS

AFTER YOU HAVE FINISHED WRITING YOUR INFORMATIVE PARAGRAPH, THINK ABOUT AND DISCUSS THESE QUESTIONS:

1. Was the graphic organizer a useful tool to help you plan before writing? Explain.

2. What supporting detail did you find most interesting? Why did you think it was interesting?

3. What understanding did you gain about how Native American life changed with the introduction of Spanish guns and horses?

SOCIAL STUDIES SKILLS | UNIT 4

Chapter 8: Dynasties of China
READING LESSON

DRAW CONCLUSIONS

LEARNING THE STRATEGY

Have you ever saved up your money to buy a special gift? If so, you probably sought out friends' opinions and read online product reviews to gather evidence to help you make a decision. This evidence helped you make an educated guess about the right gift to buy. You make these kinds of educated guesses based on evidence every day.

Historians use texts, artifacts, and other sources to gather evidence to **draw conclusions** about the past. Drawing conclusions about a text can help you figure out the author's purpose and point of view. It can also deepen your understanding of the text's content. Follow these steps to draw conclusions about a text.

> **Step 1** Read the text closely to gather evidence.
>
> **Step 2** Make educated guesses based on the evidence.
>
> **Step 3** Use the educated guesses you have made to draw a conclusion.

GUIDED MODEL

Song Landscape Paintings

Song dynasty rulers focused on peace and encouraged cultural advancements in art and literature. The Song period is especially remembered for great achievements in landscape painting.

(A) Painting changed as the Song dynasty restored order after the conflict and disorder at the end of the Tang dynasty. Early Song artists painted sweeping scenes of the harmony of the natural world. They were experiencing a time of order in government as well. Other Song painters began to paint less realistic natural scenes, showing what they felt more than what they saw.

(A) Eventually, invaders from the north forced the Song dynasty farther to the south. The Chinese began to think less about the world and more about their own local concerns. Landscape painters created smaller and more personal scenes.

Song leaders are remembered for helping China grow and become stronger. Song artists are remembered for building a strong tradition of Chinese landscape painting.

Step 1 Read the text closely to gather evidence.

EVIDENCE (A) Early Song artists painted sweeping scenes of the harmony of the natural world. Their work reflected the harmony and order in China at that time.

EVIDENCE (A) After invaders from the north entered China, the Chinese focused more on local concerns. Landscape painters created smaller and more personal scenes.

Step 2 Make educated guesses based on evidence.

EDUCATED GUESSES When there was harmony and order in their world, Song artists reflected that in their paintings. Later, when the Chinese began to focus more on local concerns, that was reflected in Song artists' paintings, too.

Step 3 Use educated guesses to draw a conclusion.

CONCLUSION Chinese landscape art changed as the state of China's government and relation to the rest of the world changed.

TIP Use a diagram to organize the evidence you have identified. Then use educated guesses to draw a conclusion. A diagram can help you clarify your thinking.

SOCIAL STUDIES SKILLS Continued

NATIONAL
GEOGRAPHIC
LEARNING

APPLYING THE STRATEGY

GETTING STARTED Now draw conclusions as you read Lesson 1.1, "Reunification Under the Sui Dynasty," in Chapter 8. As you read the lesson, use the graphic organizer below to take notes on the evidence you find and the conclusion you draw. Drawing conclusions about the text will deepen your understanding about the way in which Wendi reunified China. To get you started, one piece of evidence has been filled in for you.

COOPERATIVE OPTION You may want to show your evidence to a partner and ask that partner to draw his or her own conclusion. Compare the two conclusions, and discuss similarities and differences.

TAKING NOTES

Evidence		Conclusion
The government selected new officials by written examination and made sure they better reflected China's diverse ethnic groups.	→	
Evidence		
	→	
Evidence		
	→	

THINK AND DISCUSS

THINK ABOUT AND DISCUSS THESE QUESTIONS:

1. How did Wendi ensure that China's diverse ethnic groups would be represented?

2. What made up Wendi's new law code?

3. What conclusion can you draw about Wendi's rule?

SOCIAL STUDIES SKILLS | UNIT 4

Chapter 8: Dynasties of China
WRITING LESSON

NATIONAL GEOGRAPHIC LEARNING

WRITE AN EXPOSITORY PARAGRAPH

LEARNING THE STRATEGY

Communicating information and ideas through writing is called **expository** writing. Expository paragraphs and essays often explain an idea, tell how something works, or give information about an event or issue.

To write an expository paragraph, first select a topic. Be sure your topic is not too broad. For example, the entire history of the Grand Canal could not be explained in one paragraph. Instead, narrow your topic to cover a specific aspect of the Grand Canal. Once you've narrowed your topic, write a sentence that introduces it. This is your main idea. Then include details that support your main idea, and determine the best way to organize them. Last, conclude with a sentence that restates the main idea.

To write an expository paragraph, follow these steps.

Step 1 Select a topic you would like to inform your readers about and gather detailed information about it.

Step 2 Write a sentence that introduces and states your topic. This is your main idea.

Step 3 Include at least three details that provide information on your topic.

Step 4 Write a concluding sentence that restates your main idea in a different way.

GUIDED MODEL

(A) The Impact of the Grand Canal
(B) The impact of the Grand Canal during the Sui dynasty was immense. **(C)** The 1,200-mile Grand Canal connected the Chinese people. A road built alongside the canal carried messages back and forth between the bustling cities of Yangzhou and Beijing. **(C)** The Grand Canal also served to unite China's economy. It enabled the movement of China's extensive resources to reach government and military centers. **(C)** Finally, the canal helped transform transportation. It allowed products to be moved faster and more efficiently. **(D)** The Grand Canal was as much a marvel to the people of the Sui dynasty as GPS, smart phones, and tablets are to people of the 21st century.

Step 1 Select a topic.
  (A) The topic is the impact of the Grand Canal.

Step 2 Write a sentence that introduces and states your topic.
  (B) This sentence states the topic.

Step 3 Include at least three details that provide information on your topic.
  (C) The writer includes details on the topic.

Step 4 Write a conclusion.
  (D) The writer concludes by stating the main idea again but in a different way.

TIP Concept webs help writers brainstorm ideas. They are ideal tools to use to collect possible details to support a main idea or topic.

SOCIAL STUDIES SKILLS Continued

NATIONAL GEOGRAPHIC LEARNING

APPLYING THE STRATEGY

GETTING STARTED Now write your own expository paragraph. In the "Write About History" section of the Chapter Review, you are asked to suppose you are a historian being interviewed about China. Your task is to write an expository paragraph explaining how the Great Wall became a symbol of China's policy of isolationism at the end of the Ming dynasty. Use the steps explained in this lesson and the graphic organizer below to plan your writing. Begin by filling in your main idea. Then come up with three details that explain how the Great Wall became a symbol of isolationism. After you have organized your information, write your draft.

COOPERATIVE OPTION After you have written a draft, show it to a partner in your class and invite his or her suggestions to improve the draft. You can also offer suggestions for your partner's first draft. Remember to be positive and constructive.

TAKING NOTES

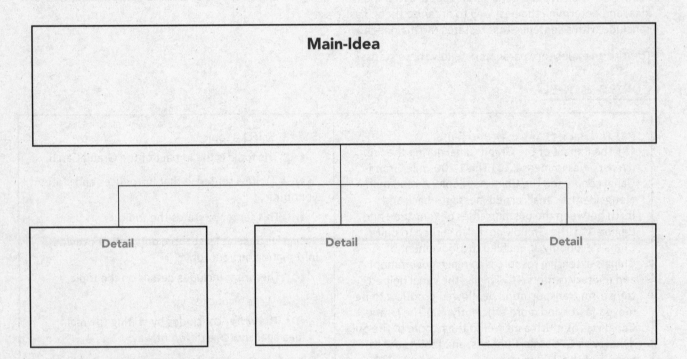

Main-Idea

Detail

Detail

Detail

THINK AND DISCUSS

AFTER YOU HAVE FINISHED WRITING YOUR EXPOSITORY PARAGRAPH, THINK ABOUT AND DISCUSS THESE QUESTIONS:

1. What was the most difficult part of your assignment?

2. What vocabulary terms did you choose? Why did you choose those terms?

3. What understanding did you gain about China's isolationism by writing the expository paragraph?

SOCIAL STUDIES SKILLS — UNIT 4

Chapter 9: Japanese Civilization
READING LESSON

MAKE INFERENCES

LEARNING THE STRATEGY

Picture this scene: A girl looks out the window with a bicycle helmet in her hands. Rain is pouring down outside, and thunder rumbles nearby. With a frown on her face, the girl puts the helmet away. You can probably infer that she wanted to go outside and ride her bicycle.

In a similar way, historians use what they know to **make inferences**, or figure out the meaning, of past events. This process helps historians analyze events. Follow these steps to make inferences and figure out the meaning of a text.

Step 1 Read the text looking for facts and ideas.

Step 2 Think about what the writer does not say but wants you to understand. Ask yourself: *How do these facts connect with what I already know? How does this information help me understand the text?*

Step 3 Reread the text and use what you know to make an inference.

GUIDED MODEL

The Mongols Attack
(A) The Mongols had already conquered China and Korea, but leader Kublai Khan wanted to control Japan, too. He launched an invasion of Japan in 1281. His forces consisted of 4,400 ships carrying about 150,000 men.

(B) The daimyo, who had been warring among themselves, put aside their differences and focused all their resources on defeating the Mongols. The Japanese warriors fought the invaders for about two months. Then a typhoon smashed into the Mongol fleet, killing tens of thousands. Japan claimed that heaven had saved the country by sending a kamikaze, or "divine wind," to stop the Mongols.

Step 1 Identify facts stated in the text.

FACT (A) The Mongol leader Kublai Khan wanted to control Japan.

Step 2 Think about what the writer does not say but wants you to understand.

UNSTATED (B) The writer doesn't explain why the daimyo put aside their differences and joined together to fight the Mongols.

Step 3 Make an inference.

INFERENCE The Japanese did not want to be controlled by the Mongols and were willing to put aside their differences to defeat the foreign invaders.

TIP Use a three-vcolumn chart to keep track of inferences. Write down facts in the first column. Write down what you already know in the second column. Write your inferences in the third column. Note that an inference can be based on one fact or several facts.

SOCIAL STUDIES SKILLS Continued

APPLYING THE STRATEGY

GETTING STARTED Now make inferences as you read Lesson 3.1, "Samurai and Shoguns," in Chapter 9. As you read the lesson, use the graphic organizer below to take notes on the inferences you make. Making inferences about the text will help you better understand the role of the samurai and shoguns in feudal Japan. One row is filled in to help you get started.

COOPERATIVE OPTION You may wish to work with a partner in your class to review the lesson and complete the graphic organizer.

TAKING NOTES

I notice...	I know...	And so...
The peasants bowed to the samurai. The samurai swore allegiance to the daimyo.	Feudal Japan had classes, or groups.	Classes in feudal Japan were ordered: peasants were below the samurai; the samurai were below the daimyo; the daimyo were leaders.

THINK AND DISCUSS

THINK ABOUT AND DISCUSS THESE QUESTIONS:

1. What can you infer about the lives of peasants in Japan at this time?

2. What role did the samurai play in Japanese feudal society?

3. What was bushido? What purpose did it serve?

WRITING LESSON

WRITE AN INFORMATIVE ARTICLE

LEARNING THE STRATEGY

When you write an informative article, you tell readers about a topic in an objective way. In other words, you inform readers without interjecting your own opinions. Let's say you want to write an article contrasting two forms of Japanese theater. Remember that when you contrast, you study differences. You could begin by introducing the topic simply: "Noh and kabuki are two forms of traditional Japanese theater that differ in many ways." This introduction states the main idea.

Next, gather information to support your main idea. For example, you might find information about when each form of theater began. Finally, you would end the text with a concluding sentence that summarizes or restates the main idea in a different way.

To write an informative article, follow these steps.

Step 1 Select a topic you would like to inform your readers about and gather detailed information about it.

Step 2 Write a sentence that introduces and states your topic. This is your main idea.

Step 3 Include at least three details on your topic.

Step 4 Write a conclusion that restates the main idea in a different way.

GUIDED MODEL

(A) Differences Between Noh and Kabuki
(B) Noh and kabuki are two forms of traditional Japanese theater that differ in many ways. **(C)** Noh began in the 1300s, while kabuki was first performed in 1603. **(C)** Noh was performed for the samurai and other members of the upper class, unlike kabuki, which appealed more to the common people. **(C)** Another difference is that stories in noh theater came from history, myth, and legend and were usually tragic. On the other hand, kabuki plays included themes of adventure, romance, feuds, and revenge. **(C)** In addition, the noh stage was simple and made of wood. The kabuki stage, on the other hand, sometimes revolved and had trapdoors. **(D)** As you can see, each form of theater had its own style, but both offered exciting entertainment for the people of Japan.

Step 1 Select a topic.

  (A) The topic is differences between noh and kabuki.

Step 2 Write a sentence that introduces and states the main idea.

  (B) This sentence states the main idea.

Step 3 Include at least three details on your topic. In this article, details have been chosen that can be compared.

  (C) The writer includes details on the topic and contrasts them.

  (D) The writer concludes by stating the main idea again but in a different way.

TIP When you research, gather more information than you need. Then choose the information that best shows differences.

SOCIAL STUDIES SKILLS Continued

NATIONAL GEOGRAPHIC LEARNING

APPLYING THE STRATEGY

GETTING STARTED Now write your own informative article. In the "Write About History" section of the Chapter Review, you are asked to write an encyclopedia article comparing or contrasting the rule of Prince Shotoku and the rule of Tokugawa Ieyasu. Use the steps explained in this lesson and the graphic organizer below to plan your informative article. The graphic organizer will help you determine your topic and organize your information. Then write a first draft.

COOPERATIVE OPTION You may want to work with a partner, with each of you gathering information on one ruler. Then you can work together to write a main idea and concluding statement and combine the information you gathered into one encyclopedia article.

TAKING NOTES

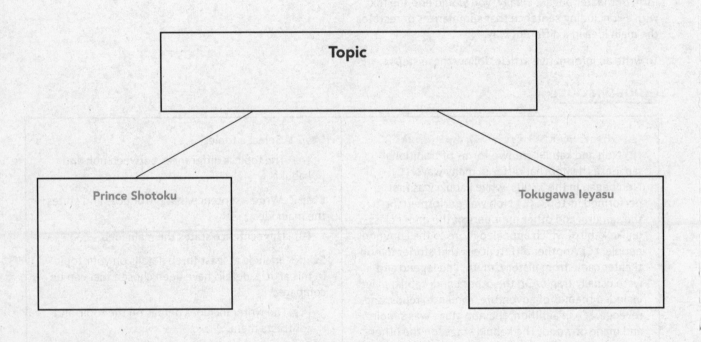

THINK AND DISCUSS

AFTER YOU HAVE FINISHED WRITING YOUR ENCYCLOPEDIA ARTICLE, THINK ABOUT AND DISCUSS THESE QUESTIONS:

1. What was one challenge you faced in writing your encyclopedia article?

2. How did you decide which details to include in your article?

3. What was the most important fact you learned about the similarities or differences between the rule of Prince Shotoku and that of Tokugawa Ieyasu?

 **SOCIAL STUDIES SKILLS | UNIT 4**   **Chapter 10: Korea, India, and Southeast Asia**
READING LESSON

 **NATIONAL GEOGRAPHIC LEARNING**

DETERMINE WORD MEANINGS

LEARNING THE STRATEGY

Sometimes when you read, you run into unfamiliar words. You could look up these words in the dictionary, but sometimes you might not have one handy, or you might not want to interrupt your reading. The alternative is to look for context clues in the text surrounding the word. Context clues are words or phrases that can help you **determine word meanings**.

Writers use context clues to define or further explain difficult or unfamiliar words. Signal words and phrases like *or, is,* and *such as* can indicate that a word is going to be defined in the text. Learning to determine word meanings will help you better understand what you read in historical texts.

To find the meaning of words from context clues, follow these steps.

Step 1 Identify an unfamiliar word.

Step 2 Read the surrounding text for context clues and signal words (*or, is, such as*) that might indicate a context clue.

Step 3 Use the context clues to determine the meaning of the word.

GUIDED MODEL

The Lost World

In 1860, French explorer Henri Mouhot encountered the "lost" world of Angkor and Angkor Wat, whose wooden structures and stone buildings had been **(A)** consumed, **(B)** or covered, by jungle after being abandoned hundreds of years earlier. Mouhot brought the site to the attention of westerners. Sadly, visitors and **(A)** looters, **(B)** or thieves, began removing its treasures.

Fortunately, in 1992, Angkor Wat became a UNESCO World Heritage Site with carefully planned measures to protect it for future generations. Today Angkor Wat is Cambodia's main tourist attraction with over two million visitors every year.

Step 1 Identify an unfamiliar word.

   UNFAMILIAR WORDS (A) consumed, looters

Step 2 Read the surrounding text looking for context clues and signal words.

   SIGNAL WORD (B) or

Step 3 Use the context clues to determine the meaning of the word.

Consumed means "covered."

Looters means "thieves."

TIP There are other signal words and phrases that can indicate a context clue. When you see words or phrases such as *called, known as,* or *meaning*, a definition or useful explanation might follow that could help you define an unfamiliar word.

SOCIAL STUDIES SKILLS Continued

NATIONAL GEOGRAPHIC LEARNING

APPLYING THE STRATEGY

GETTING STARTED Now determine the meanings of unfamiliar words and phrases in Lesson 1.4, "Korean Culture," in Chapter 10. By understanding the meaning of unfamiliar words, you'll deepen your understanding of Korean culture. Use the graphic organizer below to record the unfamiliar words you encounter, their definitions, and an example, when possible, of how the words apply to your life. Use context clues to help you determine the definitions of the words. Remember to look for signal words.

COOPERATIVE OPTION You may wish to work with a partner in your class to review the lesson and complete the graphic organizer.

TAKING NOTES

Word	Definition	Example from My Life

THINK AND DISCUSS

THINK ABOUT AND DISCUSS THESE QUESTIONS:

1. What signal words enabled you to find the meaning of some of the words?

2. How did you figure out the meaning of *painstakingly*?

3. How does knowing these words help you understand the lesson?

SOCIAL STUDIES SKILLS | UNIT 4

Chapter 10: Korea, India, and Southeast Asia
WRITING LESSON

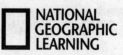
NATIONAL GEOGRAPHIC LEARNING

WRITE A NARRATIVE

LEARNING THE STRATEGY

A history text usually contains narrative accounts of events. A **narrative** is an account or story of events or experiences. Narratives may be fictional, or made up, or they may be factual. To write a historical narrative, you must understand the events, people, and places you plan to write about.

All narratives share certain characteristics, including a specific setting, or time and place. The events in a narrative usually follow a logical sequence, or order. This helps the reader understand the connections among events. Descriptive details, such as sensory details, help bring events and people to life. Sensory details are details that appeal to sight, sound, touch, taste, and smell.

Before writing a narrative, you should decide what point of view, or perspective, you will use. Most narratives are written from either a first-person or third-person point of view.

To write a narrative paragraph, follow these steps.

Step 1 Identify the topic of your narrative and gather facts about its events, people, and places.

Step 2 Determine the setting and point of view of your narrative.

Step 3 Recount events in a logical sequence.

Step 4 Use descriptive details to help bring your narrative to life.

GUIDED MODEL

(A) A Visit to Haeinsa Temple
(B) Today we are visiting Haeinsa Temple in South Korea. This is where the Tripitaka Koreana is housed. I can only imagine the painstaking effort of the monks who spent more than 16 years making and carving new wooden blocks to replace those that were burned during the Mongol invasion in 1231.

(C) As we approach the complex, I see the beautiful sloping rooftops. **(D)** The main temple is quite colorful, but the four buildings that store the wooden blocks are rather plain. But don't let looks fool you, these buildings have kept the Tripitaka Koreana in surprisingly good condition for centuries. **(D)** The floor contains a mixture of soil, charcoal, salt, clay, sand, and plaster powder that regulates moisture. Strategically placed windows of varying sizes ensure that there is a consistent air quality. These are truly preservation techniques that have stood the test of time.

Step 1 Identify the topic of your narrative.

  (A) The writer is narrating an account of a visit to Haeinsa Temple.

Step 2 Determine the setting and point of view of your narrative.

  (B) The narrative is set in modern-day South Korea at the Haeinsa Temple. The writer uses the pronouns *I* and *we* and so is employing a first-person point of view.

Step 3 Recount events in a logical sequence.

  (C) The writer takes readers through the visit in a logical sequence.

Step 4 Use descriptive details to help bring your narrative to life.

  (D) The writer uses sensory details to describe the buildings that house the Tripitaka Koreana.

TIP Use an outline to help you organize the events of your narrative and write them in a logical order.

SOCIAL STUDIES SKILLS Continued

APPLYING THE STRATEGY

GETTING STARTED Now write your own narrative. In the "Write About History" section of the Chapter Review, you are asked to suppose you are taking tourists on a tour of Angkor Wat, explaining how the structure represents the peak of Khmer artistic achievement. Use the steps explained in this lesson and the graphic organizer below to develop your narrative. Begin by creating an outline to plan your narrative. Write down key ideas after the roman numerals in the outline. Write down details after the letters in the outline. Be sure to choose descriptive details that help bring your narrative to life. Follow your outline as you draft your narrative.

COOPERATIVE OPTION After you have written a first draft, show it to a partner in your class and invite his or her suggestions to improve the draft. You can also offer suggestions for your partner's first draft. Be positive and constructive.

TAKING NOTES

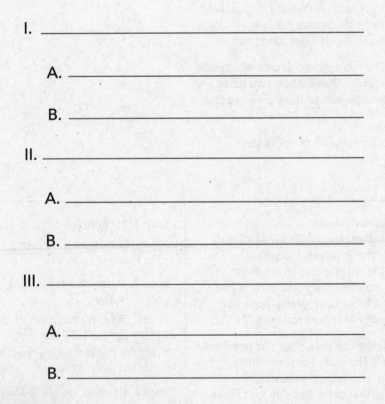

I. _____

    A. _____

    B. _____

II. _____

    A. _____

    B. _____

III. _____

    A. _____

    B. _____

THINK AND DISCUSS

AFTER YOU HAVE FINISHED WRITING YOUR NARRATIVE, THINK ABOUT AND DISCUSS THESE QUESTIONS:

1. What was one of the challenges you faced while writing the narrative?

2. How did you organize your narrative so it would work well for a tour guide taking tourists through Angkor Wat?

3. How did writing about Angkor Wat help you come to a greater understanding of the temple?

SOCIAL STUDIES SKILLS | **UNIT 5**

Chapter 11: Feudalism and the Middle Ages
READING LESSON

NATIONAL GEOGRAPHIC LEARNING

DRAW CONCLUSIONS

LEARNING THE STRATEGY

One day while you are at the public library, you see a backpack lying on the floor. The backpack is unzipped, and textbooks, pencils, and spiral-bound notebooks have spilled out of the top pocket. One of the books is a science textbook you remember reading last year. Using this evidence, you can probably guess that the person who owns the backpack is in the grade below yours. You make these kinds of educated guesses based on evidence every day.

Historians use texts, artifacts, and other sources to gather evidence and make educated guesses, or **draw conclusions**, about the past. Drawing conclusions about a text can help you figure out the author's purpose and point of view. It can also deepen your understanding of the text's content. Follow these steps to draw conclusions about a text.

Step 1 Read the text closely to gather evidence.

Step 2 Make educated guesses based on the evidence.

Step 3 Use the educated guesses you have made to draw a conclusion.

GUIDED MODEL

Social Classes in Feudal Society
The feudal system during the Middle Ages created a social order that was as tightly structured as a pyramid. **(A)** At the very top sat the king. **(A)** Next came the church officials and noblemen, who included lords and some vassals. **(A)** Lords lived in fortified castles that were guarded by knights, the third class in feudal society.

Relatively few people belonged to the upper three classes. **(A)** The great majority of people in the Middle Ages found themselves at the bottom of the social heap. This class included peasants and serfs.

Step 1 Read the text closely to gather evidence.

EVIDENCE (A) The king was at the top of feudal society.

EVIDENCE (A) Church officials and noblemen were below the king.

EVIDENCE (A) Knights made up the third class in feudal society.

EVIDENCE (A) Most people in the Middle Ages were peasants and serfs and belonged to the lowest social class.

Step 2 Make educated guesses based on evidence.

EDUCATED GUESS Social classes in feudal society were probably determined by birth.

Step 3 Use educated guesses to draw a conclusion.

CONCLUSION There was probably no way for people to improve their standing and rise to a higher level.

TIP Use a chart to organize the evidence you have identified. Then use educated guesses to draw conclusions. A chart can help you clarify your thinking.

SOCIAL STUDIES SKILLS Continued

APPLYING THE STRATEGY

GETTING STARTED Now draw conclusions as you read Lesson 1.2, "Charlemagne," in Chapter 11. As you read the lesson, use the graphic organizer below to take notes on the evidence you find. You will use this evidence to draw conclusions about Charlemagne's rule. To get you started, one piece of evidence has been filled in for you.

COOPERATIVE OPTION You may want to show your evidence to a partner and ask that partner to draw his or her own conclusion. Compare your conclusion with that of your partner and discuss similarities and differences.

TAKING NOTES

Government Policies	Religious Policies
Charlemagne wanted to unite all the Germanic kingdoms under his rule.	

THINK AND DISCUSS

THINK ABOUT AND DISCUSS THESE QUESTIONS:

1. How did Charlemagne take care of his subjects?

2. How did Charlemagne deal with those who refused to convert to Christianity?

3. What conclusions can you draw about Charlemagne's rule?

SOCIAL STUDIES SKILLS | **UNIT 5**

Chapter 11: Feudalism and the Middle Ages
WRITING LESSON

WRITING AN INFORMATIVE PARAGRAPH

LEARNING THE STRATEGY

When you write an **informative paragraph**, you tell readers about a topic in an objective way. In other words, you inform readers without interjecting your own opinions. Suppose you want to write an informative paragraph about the events that led to the signing of the Magna Carta. You could begin by introducing the topic: "A perfect storm of events led the barons to force King John to set his seal to the Magna Carta in 1215." This introduction states the main idea.

Next, include more specific information to support the main idea. For this topic, you would probably list the events that led the barons to draw up the Magna Carta and force King John to set his seal to it. You would continue to support the main idea by providing details and examples. Finally, you would end the text with a concluding sentence that summarizes or restates the main idea in a different way.

To write an informative paragraph, follow these steps.

Step 1 Select a topic you would like to inform your readers about and gather detailed information about it.

Step 2 Write a sentence that introduces and states your topic. This is your main idea.

Step 3 Include at least three details that provide information on your topic.

Step 4 Write a conclusion that restates the main idea in a different way.

GUIDED MODEL

(A) What Led to the Magna Carta
(B) A perfect storm of events led the barons to force King John to set his seal to the Magna Carta in 1215. **(C)** For one thing, King John had launched military actions in France to hold onto land that England controlled. These actions were not always successful, which disappointed the barons. They did not want to be ruled by a weak king. **(C)** Then King John raised the barons' taxes to cover the costs of the military forces. Taxes were already high, and the barons refused to pay the added amounts. **(C)** Finally, early in 1215, the barons rebelled against the king and drafted the Magna Carta to limit the ruler's authority. **(D)** On June 10, King John met with the barons at Runnymede, where he set his seal on the Magna Carta and became subject to the law of the land.

Step 1 Select a topic.
   (A) The topic is a discussion of what led to the Magna Carta.

Step 2 Write a sentence that introduces and states the main idea.
   (B) This sentence states the main idea.

Step 3 Include at least three details that provide information on your topic.
   (C) The writer includes details on the topic.

Step 4 Write a concluding sentence.
   (D) The writer concludes by stating the main idea again but in a different way.

TIP Gather as many details as you can and list them in a Main Idea and Details chart. Then number the details in the order that you think will be the most effective.

SOCIAL STUDIES SKILLS Continued

APPLYING THE STRATEGY

GETTING STARTED Now write your own informative paragraph. In the "Write About History" section of the Chapter Review, you are asked to write a paragraph for a children's encyclopedia, informing readers about the events that brought about the downfall of feudalism and the Middle Ages. Use the steps explained in this lesson and the graphic organizer below to plan your informative writing. The graphic organizer will help you organize your main idea and details. After you have determined your main idea and details, write your draft.

COOPERATIVE OPTION After you have written your draft, show it to a partner in your class and invite his or her suggestions on ways to improve the draft. You can also offer suggestions for your partner's draft. Remember to be positive and constructive.

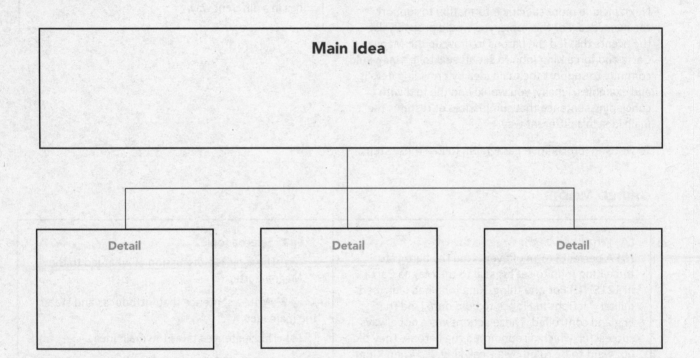

THINK AND DISCUSS

AFTER YOU HAVE FINISHED WRITING YOUR INFORMATIVE PARAGRAPH, THINK ABOUT AND DISCUSS THESE QUESTIONS:

1. What was one challenge you faced in writing your informative paragraph?

2. What supporting detail did you find most interesting? Why did you think it was interesting?

3. What understanding about the downfall of feudalism and the Middle Ages did you gain by writing the paragraph?

SOCIAL STUDIES SKILLS UNIT 5

Chapter 12: Renaissance and Reformation
READING LESSON

NATIONAL GEOGRAPHIC LEARNING

ANALYZE LANGUAGE USE

LEARNING THE STRATEGY

Have you ever seen an animated movie with animal characters that speak and act like humans? Giving human qualities to something that isn't human is called personification. Personification is a type of figurative language. Figurative language is language that describes something by comparing it to something else. Other types of figurative language include similes and metaphors.

Writers use figurative language to play with language and to provide readers with comparisons that may help them think of things in a different way. Good readers **analyze language use** to determine not only the literal meaning but also the figurative meaning of words and phrases the writer uses.

To analyze the language use in a text, follow these steps.

Step 1 Identify examples of figurative language in the text.

Step 2 Analyze the comparison to understand its meaning.

Step 3 Determine how the language use indicates the author's tone and purpose.

GUIDED MODEL

The Printing Press
(A) Today, ideas can fly around the world at the push of a button or the click of a mouse. In the early days of the Renaissance, however, ideas mostly spread by word of mouth as traders and travelers made their slow way from place to place. But then Johann Gutenberg, a German printer, came up with an invention that sped up the exchange of ideas. **(A)** In many ways, it was the Internet of its day. The invention was the printing press.

Around the same time, a new technique for making paper was developed, which made paper easier to manufacture. Gutenberg used this paper and his new press to print a Latin Bible. He tried to keep his printing technique a secret, but his beautiful Bible caught people's attention. **(A)** The technology of the new printing press spread as quickly as wildfire.

Step 1 Identify examples of figurative language.
  (A) These sentences include figurative language.

Step 2 Analyze the comparison to understand its meaning.
Ideas spread so quickly they seem to "fly."
The printing press spread ideas more quickly than ever before.
The printing press was very popular.

Step 3 Determine how word choice indicates the author's purpose.
Using the word *fly* helps readers understand the author is implying quickness.
Comparing the printing press to the Internet lets readers know how important the printing press was in its day for relaying information.
Using the word *wildfire* helps readers understand how quickly the technology spread.

TIP As you read, jot down interesting or unfamiliar word choices to analyze later.

SOCIAL STUDIES SKILLS Continued

APPLYING THE STRATEGY

GETTING STARTED Now try analyzing language use in Lesson 1.4, "The Medici and the Borgias," in Chapter 12. As you read the lesson, use the graphic organizer below to take notes on the language used to describe the Medici and the Borgias. To get you started, one example of figurative language has already been filled in for you in the main circle. In the smaller circles, write down its meaning, tone, and purpose.

COOPERATIVE OPTION Work with a partner to complete the graphic organizer. Then find other examples of figurative language in the text.

TAKING NOTES

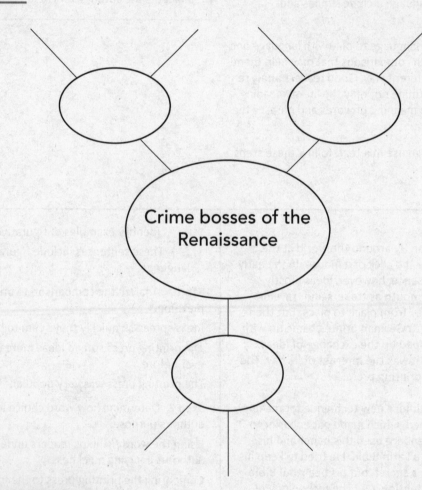

Crime bosses of the Renaissance

THINK AND DISCUSS

THINK ABOUT AND DISCUSS THESE QUESTIONS:

1. What does the author mean by describing the Medici as the "crime bosses of the Renaissance"?

2. What tone do the words convey?

3. Why do you think the author used these words to describe the Medici?

SOCIAL STUDIES
SKILLS | UNIT **5** | Chapter 12: Renaissance and Reformation
WRITING LESSON

NATIONAL
GEOGRAPHIC
LEARNING

WRITE AN EXPLANATORY TEXT

LEARNING THE STRATEGY

When you write an **explanatory text**, you give readers information about a topic. You provide facts and examples so they will understand the topic more fully. Types of explanatory writing include newspaper articles, textbooks, encyclopedia entries, and how-to articles.

To write an explanatory text, first select a topic. For example, suppose you have an assignment to write a paragraph about the advances in science during the Renaissance. You'd start by writing a sentence that introduces the topic. This is your main idea. Then you would include details that support your main idea. Next you would consider how best to organize your details. Last, you would conclude with a sentence that restates the main idea.

To write an explanatory text, follow these steps.

Step 1 Select a topic you would like to inform your readers about and gather detailed information about it.

Step 2 Write a sentence that introduces and states your topic. This is your main idea.

Step 3 Include at least three details that provide information on your topic.

Step 4 Write a concluding sentence about your topic that restates the main idea in a different way.

GUIDED MODEL

(A) Scientific Advances During the Renaissance
(B) The Renaissance greatly influenced the arts and architecture, but it made its mark on the sciences as well. **(C)** Renaissance thinkers became interested in the natural world. Some scientists learned about the metals and minerals that make up Earth's surface. **(C)** Others studied astronomy and gained a new understanding of the wider universe and Earth's place in it. **(C)** Scientific ideas were also applied to cartography, or mapmaking. Using these new ideas, exploration by men such as Christopher Columbus continued to improve the accuracy of maps. **(D)** These advances in science paved the way for new understandings about the world, many of which are still felt today.

Step 1 Select a topic.
   (A) The topic is scientific advances during the Renaissance.

Step 2 Write a sentence that introduces and states your topic.
   (B) This sentence states the topic.

Step 3 Include at least three details that provide information on your topic.
   (C) The writer includes details on the topic.

Step 4 Write a concluding sentence.
   (D) The writer concludes by stating the main idea again but in a different way.

TIP Think about the best way to organize your details for your readers. Determine what makes the most sense for your topic. You could organize information chronologically, in numbered steps, or in categories.

SOCIAL STUDIES SKILLS Continued

NATIONAL GEOGRAPHIC LEARNING

APPLYING THE STRATEGY

GETTING STARTED Now write your own explanatory text. In the "Write About History" section of the Chapter Review, you are asked to write an explanatory paragraph informing museumgoers about the ways in which Renaissance ideas changed Europe. Use the steps explained in this lesson and the graphic organizer below to plan your paragraph. Begin by filling in your main idea. Then come up with three details that explain the ways in which Renaissance ideas changed Europe. After you have organized your information, write your draft.

COOPERATIVE OPTION After you have written a first draft, show it to a partner in your class and invite his or her suggestions to improve the draft. You can also offer suggestions for your partner's first draft. Remember to be positive and constructive.

TAKING NOTES

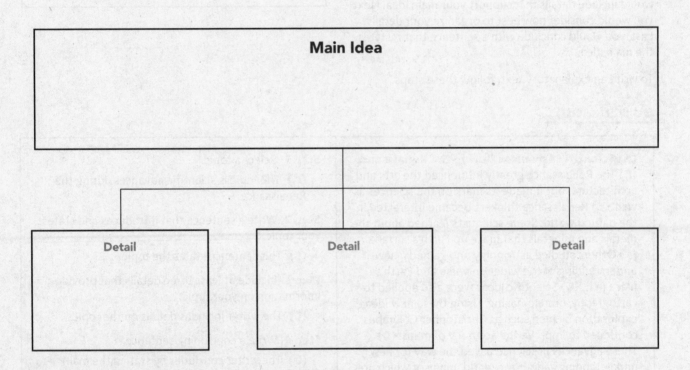

Main Idea

| Detail | Detail | Detail |

THINK AND DISCUSS

AFTER YOU HAVE FINISHED WRITING YOUR PARAGRAPH, THINK ABOUT AND DISCUSS THESE QUESTIONS:

1. What was one of the challenges you faced in writing your explanatory paragraph?

2. What do you think was the most important effect of the Renaissance on Europe? What evidence from the text makes you think so?

3. What understanding about the Renaissance did you gain by writing the explanatory paragraph?

SOCIAL STUDIES SKILLS | UNIT 5

Chapter 13: The Age of Science and Exploration
READING LESSON

NATIONAL GEOGRAPHIC LEARNING

MAKE INFERENCES

LEARNING THE STRATEGY

Suppose it's dinnertime. You arrive home, walk through the door, and smell something delicious. You were already hungry, and this smell makes you even hungrier. Although you haven't yet entered the kitchen, you can probably assume that dinner is cooking.

In a similar way, historians use what they know to **make inferences**, or figure out the meaning, of past events. This process helps historians analyze events. Follow these steps to make inferences and figure out the meaning of a text.

Step 1 Read the text looking for facts and ideas.

Step 2 Think about what the writer does not say but wants you to understand. Ask yourself: *How do these facts connect with what I already know? How does this information help me understand the text?*

Step 3 Reread the text and use what you know to make an inference.

GUIDED MODEL

The Push to Trade

The Renaissance encouraged a spirit of adventure and inspired curiosity about the world. Western Europe's population was booming. **(A)** Above all, merchants were impatient to find new trading opportunities—and new markets.

In the 1400s, many of Europe's most valuable luxuries, including silk and spices, came from Asia. However, the Ottoman Empire controlled the trade routes. **(A)** Europe's leaders and merchants wanted a share of this profitable trade, so they sponsored numerous sailing expeditions to search for an alternative sea route to Asia. **(B)** By 1450, important advances in shipbuilding had made longer sea journeys possible.

Step 1 Identify facts stated in the text.

    FACT (A) Merchants wanted to find new trading opportunities.

    FACT (A) Europe's leaders and merchants wanted to participate in trade, so they sponsored sailing expeditions.

Step 2 Think about what the writer does not say but wants you to understand.

    UNSTATED (B) The writer doesn't explain what motivated advances in shipbuilding.

Step 3 Make an inference.

INFERENCE Advances made in shipbuilding were motivated by the desire of Europe's leaders and merchants to gain a share of the trade routes.

TIP Use a two-column chart to keep track of inferences. Write facts that you learned in the first column. Write your inferences in the second column. Note that an inference can be based on one fact or several facts.

SOCIAL STUDIES SKILLS Continued

APPLYING THE STRATEGY

GETTING STARTED Now make inferences as you read Lesson 3.2, "Portugal's Empire," in Chapter 13. As you read the lesson, use the graphic organizer below to take notes on the inferences you make. Making inferences about the text will help you better understand how maritime exploration and trade helped Portugal become a powerful empire. One row is filled in to help you get started.

COOPERATIVE OPTION You may wish to work with a partner in your class to review the lesson and complete the graphic organizer.

TAKING NOTES

I Learned	My Inference
Portugal tapped into the spice trade with Asia.	Spices were highly valued.

THINK AND DISCUSS

THINK ABOUT AND DISCUSS THESE QUESTIONS:

1. How did a focus on maritime exploration and trade lead Portugal to develop a powerful commercial empire?

2. Why do you think Muslim merchants did not welcome Portuguese traders?

3. What can you infer about the Portuguese rulers' attitudes toward slaves?

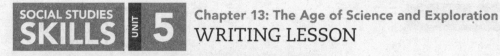

SOCIAL STUDIES
SKILLS UNIT **5**

Chapter 13: The Age of Science and Exploration
WRITING LESSON

NATIONAL
GEOGRAPHIC
LEARNING

WRITE AN INFORMATIVE PARAGRAPH

LEARNING THE STRATEGY

When you write an **informative paragraph**, you tell readers about a topic in an objective way. In other words, you inform readers without interjecting your own opinions. Suppose you want to write an informative paragraph about Isaac Newton's contributions to science. You could begin by introducing the topic: "The English scientist Isaac Newton expanded scientific understanding of the universe in the 1600s." This introduction states the main idea.

Next, include more specific information to support the main idea. For example, you might explain that Isaac Newton proposed the law of universal gravitation. You would continue to support the main idea by providing more details and examples. Finally, you would end the text with a concluding sentence that summarizes or restates the main idea in a different way.

To write an informative paragraph, follow these steps.

Step 1 Select a topic you would like to inform your readers about and gather detailed information about it.

Step 2 Write a sentence that introduces and states your topic. This is your main idea.

Step 3 Include at least three details that provide information on your topic.

Step 4 Write a conclusion that restates the main idea in a different way.

GUIDED MODEL

(A) How Isaac Newton Advanced Science
(B) The English scientist Isaac Newton expanded scientific understanding of the universe in the 1600s. **(C)** He proposed the law of universal gravitation, which holds that all objects in the universe attract one another. **(C)** With this law and his three laws of motion, Newton created a complete mechanical explanation of motion in the universe. **(C)** The Royal Society of London, an organization dedicated to advancing and sharing scientific knowledge, helped spread Newton's ideas. **(D)** His work would provide the foundation of modern physics and lead to scientific advances ranging from steam engines to space rockets.

Step 1 Select a topic.
  (A) The topic is how Isaac Newton advanced science.

Step 2 Write a sentence that introduces and states the main idea.
  (B) This sentence states the main idea.

Step 3 Include at least three details that provide information on your topic.
  (C) The writer includes details on the topic.

Step 4 Write a concluding sentence.
  (D) The writer concludes by stating the main idea again but in a different way.

TIP Gather as many details as you can and list them in a Main Idea and Details chart. Then number the details in the order that you think will be the most effective.

SOCIAL STUDIES SKILLS Continued

APPLYING THE STRATEGY

GETTING STARTED Now write your own informative paragraph. In the "Write About History" section of the Chapter Review, you are asked to write an informative paragraph for other students explaining how scientific rationalism changed Europeans' basic approach to science. Use the steps explained in this lesson and the graphic organizer below to plan your informative paragraph. The graphic organizer will help you organize your main idea and details. After you have determined your main idea and details, write your draft.

COOPERATIVE OPTION After you have written a first draft, read it aloud to a partner. Ask for his or her constructive suggestions to improve the draft. Then listen to your partner's informative paragraph and offer constructive comments.

TAKING NOTES

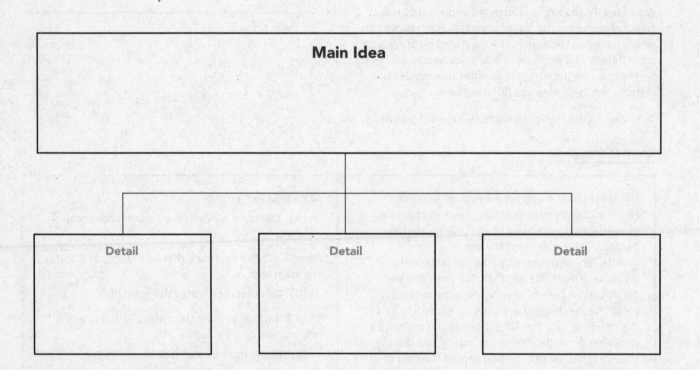

THINK AND DISCUSS

AFTER YOU HAVE FINISHED WRITING YOUR INFORMATIVE PARAGRAPH, THINK ABOUT AND DISCUSS THESE QUESTIONS:

1. How did you decide which details to include in your paragraph?

2. What model did you use for your concluding sentence? Why?

3. What was the most important idea you learned about how scientific rationalism affected Europeans' approach to science?

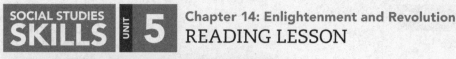

Chapter 14: Enlightenment and Revolution
READING LESSON

DETERMINE WORD MEANINGS

LEARNING THE STRATEGY

When you read, you probably come across unfamiliar words from time to time. You may find them in news stories, magazine articles, or books that you read for fun. When you read history texts, you most likely encounter unfamiliar words related to people, places, ideas, and events.

Learning to **determine word meanings** will help you better understand what you read in historical texts. One way to determine word meanings is to look at word parts, such as prefixes, suffixes, and root words. You can also think of similar words that you already know and use context clues to figure out a word's meaning. Use the following steps to determine the meanings of unfamiliar words.

> **Step 1** As you read the text, identify unfamiliar words.
>
> **Step 2** Use word parts, similar words, and context clues to help you determine word meanings.

GUIDED MODEL

Enlightened Rulers

To understand why Enlightenment thinkers argued that people should have rights and freedoms, it is important to know how governments changed over time in Europe. In medieval Europe, **(A)** influential groups such as the nobility and the Church limited the power of kings and queens. As medieval order broke down, however, monarchs took more power for themselves. By 1600, some ruled as absolute monarchs. They had unlimited authority and almost no legal limits. They claimed to rule by **(A)** divine right, meaning that their power came directly from God.

Joseph II of Austria oversaw enlightened reforms between 1780 and 1790. He introduced religious tolerance, freedom of the press, and various law reforms. Joseph firmly believed in social equality. He **(A)** promoted elementary education for all children. He put an end to serfdom and tried to introduce a new system of taxes on the land that would be more fair to different social classes.

Step 1 Identify unfamiliar words.

Step 2 Use word parts, similar words, and context clues to help you determine word meanings.

(A) *Influential* is similar to the word *influence*, which means "to have an impact on." I think that an influential group is one that has the power to influence others.

(A) Context clues in this sentence tell me that *divine* means "coming from God."

(A) *Promoted* has the prefix *pro-*, which means "in favor of." Since Joseph II promoted elementary education for all children, that must mean that he was in favor of it.

TIP Use a word map to help you determine the meaning of unfamiliar words. You can refer to your word map when you need to review vocabulary terms.

SOCIAL STUDIES SKILLS Continued

NATIONAL GEOGRAPHIC LEARNING

APPLYING THE STRATEGY

GETTING STARTED Now determine the meanings of unfamiliar words in Lesson 2.1, "The American Revolution," in Chapter 14. Determining the meanings of unfamiliar words in this lesson will deepen your understanding of how the American fight for independence reflected Enlightenment ideals. Use the graphic organizer below to record the first unfamiliar word you encounter. Identify the word parts, similar words, or context clues that helped you determine the word's meaning. Then write its definition in the appropriate place in the graphic organizer. Create a new graphic organize for each unfamiliar word you come across.

COOPERATIVE OPTION You may wish to work with a partner in your class to review the lesson and complete your graphic organizers.

TAKING NOTES

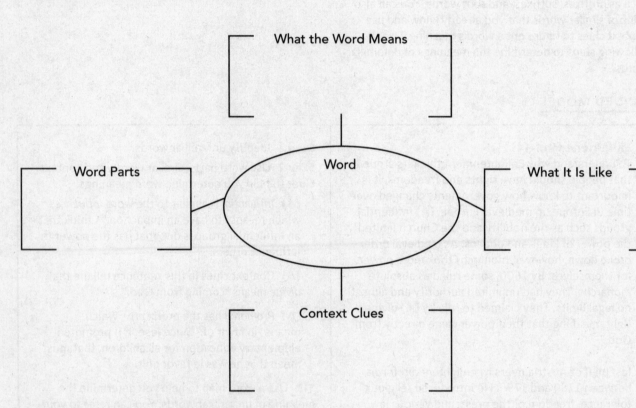

What the Word Means

Word Parts

Word

What It Is Like

Context Clues

THINK AND DISCUSS

THINK ABOUT AND DISCUSS THESE QUESTIONS:

1. What words are similar to *declaration*?

2. What context clues tell you that *prevailed* means "won"?

3. How does knowing the meaning of the root word *rebel* help you understand the meaning of *rebellion*?

Chapter 14: Enlightenment and Revolution
WRITING LESSON

WRITE AN EXPOSITORY TEXT

LEARNING THE STRATEGY

Communicating information and ideas through writing is called **expository** writing. An expository text often explains an idea, tells how something works, or gives information about an event or issue.

To write an expository text, first select a topic. Be sure your topic is not too broad. For example, if you decided to write about Mary Wollstonecraft, you would probably choose a specific aspect of her work, such as her support of equal rights in education for women. Once you've narrowed your topic, write a sentence that introduces it. This is your main idea. Then include details that support your main idea, and determine the best way to organize them. Last, conclude with a sentence that restates the main idea.

To write an expository paragraph, follow these steps.

Step 1 Select a topic you would like to inform your readers about and gather detailed information about it.

Step 2 Write a sentence that introduces and states your topic. This is your main idea.

Step 3 Include at least three details that provide information on your topic.

Step 4 Write a concluding sentence that restates your main idea in a different way.

GUIDED MODEL

(A) Mary Wollstonecraft's Support for Equal Rights in Women's Education
(B) Mary Wollstonecraft supported equality in education for women. **(C)** In 1784, she helped start a school for girls in a London suburb. **(C)** Three years later, she published her first book, *Thoughts on the Education of Daughters*. In this book, she argued that giving girls the same education as boys, instead of just training them in the social graces, would make them better mothers and citizens.

Her most famous work, *A Vindication of the Rights of Woman*, was published in 1792. **(C)** In this book, Wollstonecraft argued that a lack of educational opportunities kept women from showing their true potential. **(D)** Her calls for women to be educated equally alongside men inspired women to seek greater opportunities.

Step 1 Select a topic.
   (A) The topic is Mary Wollstonecraft's support for equal rights in women's education.

Step 2 Write a sentence that introduces and states your topic.
   (B) This sentence states the topic.

Step 3 Include at least three details that provide information on your topic.
   (C) The writer includes details on the topic.

Step 4 Write a conclusion.
   (D) The writer concludes by stating the main idea again but in a different way.

TIP Concept webs help writers brainstorm ideas. They are ideal tools to use to collect possible details to support a main idea or topic.

SOCIAL STUDIES SKILLS Continued

NATIONAL GEOGRAPHIC LEARNING

APPLYING THE STRATEGY

GETTING STARTED Now write your own expository text. In the "Write About History" section of the Chapter Review, you are asked to write a speech for an Independence Day celebration explaining how the Enlightenment helped shape the government and society we have today. Use the steps explained in this lesson and the graphic organizer below to plan your writing. Begin by filling in your main idea. Then come up with three details that explain how the Enlightenment has influenced our government and society. After you have organized your information, draft your speech.

COOPERATIVE OPTION After you have written a draft, show it to a partner in your class and invite his or her suggestions to improve the draft. You can also offer suggestions for your partner's first draft. Remember to be positive and constructive.

TAKING NOTES

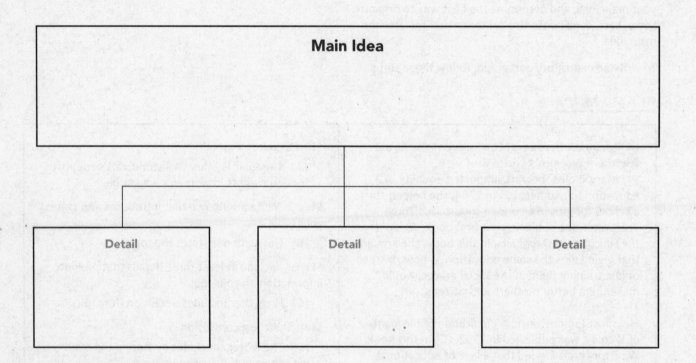

Main Idea

Detail   Detail   Detail

THINK AND DISCUSS

AFTER YOU HAVE FINISHED WRITING YOUR SPEECH, THINK ABOUT AND DISCUSS THESE QUESTIONS:

1. What was one of the challenges you faced in writing your speech?

2. What vocabulary terms did you choose? Why did you choose those terms?

3. What understanding about the influence of the Enlightenment did you gain by writing the speech?